HOME LIFE:

TWELVE LECTURES.

BY

WILLIAM HAGUE, D.D

PHILADELPHIA:
AMERICAN BAPTIST PUBLICATION SOCIETY,
No. 530 ARCH STREET.

TO THE

MEMORY OF MY SON,

John Moriarty Hague,

WHO,

ON THE 31ST OF OCTOBER, 1854, AT THE AGE OF

TWENTY YEARS AND THREE MONTHS,

WAS CALLED AWAY

FROM THE SCENES OF EARTH TO HIS HOME IN HEAVEN

This Volume

IS

DEDICATED.

Contents.

LECTURE IV.

DUTIES OF PARENTS TO CHILDREN.

"Train up a child in the way he should go, and when he is old he will not depart from it."—PROVERBS xxii. 6.

LECTURE V.

DUTIES OF CHILDREN TO PARENTS.

"Children, obey your parents in the Lord: for this is right. Honor thy father and mother, (which is the first commandment with promise,) that it may be well with thee, and thou mayest live long on the earth."—EPHESIANS vi. 1, 2, 3.

LECTURE VI.

DUTIES OF BROTHERS AND SISTERS.

"Behold how good and how pleasant it is for brethren to dwell together in unity."—PSALM cxxxiii. 1.

LECTURE VII.

MUTUAL DUTIES OF HOUSEHOLDERS AND SERVANTS.

"Thou shalt not oppress a hired servant that is poor and needy, whether he be of thy brethren, or of the strangers of thy land within thy gates."—DEUTERONOMY xxiv. 14.

LECTURE VIII.

DUTIES OF PRINCIPALS TO CLERKS AND APPRENTICES.

"Happy are thy men, happy are these thy servants."—1 KINGS x. 8.

LECTURE IX.

LECTURE X.

LECTURE XI.

LECTURE XII.

The Marriage Institution.

"MARRIAGE IS HONORABLE IN ALL."
Hebrews xiii. 4.

" How small of all that human hearts endure
That part which laws or kings can cause or cure !
Still to ourselves in every place consign'd,
Our own felicity we make or find :
With secret course, which no loud storms annoy,
Glides the smooth current of domestic joy."

THIS fine sentiment, which Goldsmith has so well expressed, was suggested to the poet by a wide and close survey of society, as it disclosed itself to the curious eye of a philosophic traveller. He had looked upon every phase of European life with a genial, sympathetic spirit; he had been welcomed as a friend and companion by men and children of every rank and station; he had participated in the joys and sorrows of the noble and the peasant; had felt himself at home alike in the turretted castle and the thatched hut; and yet, in spite of all the diversified contrasts that are caused by wealth and poverty, he exults in the cheering truth that every man's happiness is committed chiefly to his own keeping, because real happiness springs from deep interior sources, which the caprices of Fortune or Power cannot destroy. He had witnessed, no doubt, strange sights of splendid misery as well as of abject wretchedness; but often, in the lowly cottage which Love, Chastity, and Honor had hallowed as a home of the heart, he had seen the signs of that mental peace, and of that healthful play of kind affections, which the lordly proprietor of the neighboring domain might have sighed in vain to possess.

Amidst all the desolating changes, the cares and pains of this disordered world, what reason have we to thank God that we are greeted on every side by some reminiscences of Paradise! that when man was banished from scenes of primeval bliss, he bore with him two divine institutions, as memorials of his "first estate," as lights and aids to cheer the gloom of his exile, and to awaken hopes of a better day! We speak of the Sabbath and Marriage, for both are tokens of God's love, and of his paternal interest in the moral welfare of our fallen race. Our Saviour declared that "the Sabbath was made for man"—that is, adapted to his physical and moral wants. So, too, marriage was made for man by Him who said in the beginning, from a regard to the social nature which He had created, "It is not good for man to be alone," and who enstamped perpetual dignity on the institution, when, amidst the bowers and bloom of Eden, He presented the first bride to her husband.

The marriage institution has been aptly designated "the hinge of all kindred, the capital link of the chain that binds society together." In all ages of the world, it has been regarded as of divine origin. The beautiful old chant of the Jewish Temple-service sounded out the truth, which has been acknowledged in almost every nation of the earth: "God setteth the solitary in families." Without the institution of marriage, the family could have had no existence; and without the family there could have been no ties of kindred, no social order, no growth of private affections, no source of public virtue, no civilization, and no progress. Every human being, bereft of domestic relations, would exist in a state of savage solitude, and the social condition of the world would realize anew that terrible description of the antediluvian age, which the pen of Moses has transmitted to us:" the earth was corrupt before God, and the earth was filled with violence."

Regarding, then, the marriage institution as the primary source of all friendly relationships, of all "the tender charities of life," the bulwark of virtue, peace, and order, let us proceed to consider,

I. THE FOUNDATION UPON WHICH IT RESTS.

II. SEVERAL PRACTICAL LESSONS WHICH THE SUBJECT SUGGESTS.

In regard to the foundation of the marriage institution, speculative philosophers have propounded various theories which cannot endure the test of sober examination. Some of these theories are treated with due respect when they are designated as mental vagaries. They seem to have been suggested by a spirit of hostility to all the restraints of law upon the spontaneous play of appetite and passion, rather than by the spirit of sound philosophy. They have been announced by individuals, by cliques and schools and socialistic organizations, whose chief aim has been to break the bands of the marriage covenant, and treat its obligations with contempt; to degrade woman from her proper rank as the wedded equal and companion of man, and to render her the mere instrument of his pleasure, the toy of caprice. They have aimed their most malignant shafts against marriage, in view of the same reasons for which Milton celebrated it in his animated strain:

> Hail, wedded love! mysterious law! true source
> Of human offspring! sole propriety
> In Paradise, if all things common else!
> By thee adulterous lust was driven from man,
> Among the bestial herds to range; by thee,
> (Founded in reason, loyal, just, and pure,)
> Relations dear, and all the charities
> Of father, son, and brother, first were known.

They have asserted that the institution is founded in superstition, or in priestcraft,—in the prejudice which defends old customs, or in some form of conventionalism. Poor, superficial absurdity! As if such shifting quicksands could have sustained the weight of the social structure as it has long stood amongst the civilized nations—unmoved amidst the drifting wrecks of empires, amidst the changes of national creeds, and in spite of the advancement of human knowledge! An institution which has put forth such a mighty power to modify the whole form of human society, to curb and guide the strongest passions of our nature,—an institution which has endured the shocks of those moral convulsions that have shaken the world, and still keeps its hold as firmly as ever upon the consciences and hearts of mankind, must surely rest upon some deep and rocky foundations very different from any that could have been furnished by the conventional arrangements of patriarchal times. The old childish story, that the world stands on the back of an elephant, contains as much of sober sense, touching the relation of effect and cause, as this class of theories exhibits touching the basis of the marriage institution.

But now, when we regard this institution as a great fact of history, and address ourselves to the work of finding out some method by which we may account for its existence, its power, and authority, the inquiring and reflecting mind can rest with satisfaction in no view of its origin, except that which is set forth by our Saviour himself, who declared marriage to be an appointment of God, forecast in the plan of creation, and founded, therefore, in the constitution of nature. "Have ye not read," said he, "that He who made them at the beginning made them male and female, and said, For this cause shall a man leave father and mother, and shall cleave to his wife, and they twain shall be one flesh? Wherefore they are no more twain, but one flesh. What, therefore, God hath joined together, let not man put asunder." This declaration of our great Teacher is in perfect harmony with the teachings of history and of philosophy. For if, for a moment, we set the authority of a divine revelation entirely out of view, what is the conclusion to which a sober philosophy will conduct us? What "doth nature itself teach" us? Reasoning from facts, we learn surely as much as this: that the *existence* and the *regulation* of the social propensities and passions are both essential to the preservation of the human race. If there were not such propensities in existence, universal celibacy would lead to the extinction of our species. But then, while we perceive that these propensities are essential elements of our being, we also perceive that an utterly lawless or unrestrained indulgence of them would lead to the ultimate extinction of the race as certainly, although not as speedily, as universal celibacy. Either the annihilation of these propensities on the one hand, or the blindly impulsive indulgence of them on the other, would violate the natural law of self-preservation. Hence it follows that these great moving forces of human nature must be guided by some well-defined rule, and their sphere of action restricted within some proper limit. While the absolute necessity of *some* such limitation is obvious to the view of all, the lights of reason and of experience unite in showing that a law of limitation can be placed on no ground whatsoever, so that it shall have authority and moral force, except in that permanent union of the sexes which God himself has enjoined, dignified, and blessed, in the establishment of the marriage institution.

Reposing on these deep and strong foundations, this sacred institution will remain unshaken by all the assaults of unbridled passion and by all the schemings of infidel philosophy. Every plea that we utter in its behalf is but an echo of the teaching of nature, and we only repeat the lessons which the voice of nature sounds forth in the ears of all mankind—lessons illustrated by the health, strength, and wealth, the domestic peace, the scenes of comfort, the civil benefits and the moral progress which are the heritage of those who observe this great fundamental law; illustrated, too, by the nameless ills and woes, the wasting diseases, the languor of natural affections, the destruction of every element that enters into the composition of home life, by the death of neglected offspring, by the utter disorganization of the social state, and by the fell swoop of rampant vices that have darkened the history of every household, and of every neighborhood, and of every community, wherein this ordinance of Heaven has been dishonored.

And here, while we are speaking of the marriage law as a part of the constitution of nature, and while we see in this unity a beautiful harmony between the teaching of reason and revelation, let it be observed that POLYGAMY is as directly opposed to the laws of nature as it is to the laws of the Bible and of all Christian nations. For the substantial equality of the numbers of both sexes born, in all countries, at all times, and amidst every diversity of circumstances, proves that it is the divine plan, as Paul expresses it, that "every man should have his own wife, and every woman her own husband;" that is, that single individuals should be exclusively united. An unequal distribution is, evidently, not "the intention of nature;" and therefore, to use the words of the celebrated

Spurzheim, "polygamy is in opposition to the natural law of morality;" * it is suited only to the genius of those old oriental despotisms under whose shelter it has thriven, whose rapacious passions it has nourished, and whose power it is gradually consuming.

The argument which I have just announced, touching the will of God, expressed in the constitution of nature, is, in effect, brought clearly to view by the prophet Malachi, (chap. ii. 14, 15,) who taught that if it had been God's design to allow a man to have more wives than one, He would have originally created more women than men. In one of his bold remonstances against the sins of his times, he exclaims, "The Lord hath been witness between thee and the wife of thy youth, against whom thou hast dealt treacherously. Yet is she thy companion, and the wife of thy covenant. And did not he make one? Yet had he the residue of the Spirit. And wherefore one? That he might seek a godly seed. Therefore take heed to your spirit, and let none deal treacherously against the wife of his youth." Two far-reaching truths are here asserted by the last of the Old Testament prophets 1. That God laid the foundation of the marriage institution in the original creation of a single pair; 2. That the benign aim of this arrangement was the advancement of human happiness, by the cultivation of religion and virtue in the family.

And here, surely, in the case of every reflecting and

---

* Spurzheim's Philosophical Catechism on the Natural Laws of Man, p. 85.

candid reader, who has had fair opportunities for observing the varied aspects of human society, we may safely appeal to those calm judgments which such an observation has suggested. Where is the man, gifted with ordinary means of information, who has not seen that, wheresoever the sanctions of the marriage institution are disregarded, home life has no permanent attractions; that the private virtues of every class are deprived of all genial aliment; that there domestic education cannot exist, and the evil passions of childhood are left to luxuriate in fearful wildness; that there the kindly affections of our nature are often blasted in the bud; that habits of industry and of self-control are never formed, and the moral dignity of woman—that great conservative element of the social state—can scarcely be named but to awaken the ruthless spirit of mockery and satire? Entirely truthful to nature and to history are the words of Robert Hall, in his celebrated discourse on Modern Infidelity: "Marriage institutions are the great civilizers of the world, and essential to the welfare of mankind. They are sources of tenderness as well as guardians of peace. Without the permanent union of sexes there can be no permanent union of families; the dissolution of nuptial ties involves the dissolution of domestic society. But domestic society is the seminary of social affections, the cradle of sensibility, where the first elements are acquired of that tenderness and humanity which cement mankind together; and were they entirely extinguished, the whole fabric of social institutions would be dissolved." What a signal realization of this truth was presented to the gaze of all mankind by the most refined country of Europe, during that "Reign of Terror" which covered the whole realm with a pall of funereal gloom! Although the French Revolution sprang, by a natural law of reäction, from the atrocities of that kingly and priestly despotism that had preceded it, nevertheless, it became a raging whirlwind, which the Genius of Infidelity could not rule; and when we pore over the horrors of that stormy time, when our hearts sicken in view of that chaotic ruin into which France was plunged, let us remember that this state of things was heralded by the granting of twenty thousand divorces in the city of Paris in a single year, and celebrated by the public adoration of a beautiful, but vile and shameless woman, who was enthroned as the "Goddess of Reason," and borne through the streets in a splendid chariot, amid the honors of a grand triumphal procession. Facts like these have a terrible significance, showing, as they do, to what an extent the moral sentiment had become corrupted throughout all classes of a cultivated community, and showing, too, that wheresoever the marriage institution—the chief support of domestic virtue—becomes subverted, the state itself will reel from its position, and involve all the interests of society in its overthrow. No wonder is it that, at a later period, Napoleon, with that keen intuition which distinguished him, declared it as his opinion that the great want of France was a new race of mothers. What deep and solemn meanings lay enfolded in that sentence! Was it possible for mortal lips, in words so few, to pay a finer tribute to the dignity of that institution of which we speak, ordained of Heaven, as it is, to be the basis upon which shall rest the whole fabric of domestic happiness, of social order, of a vital and progressive civilization?

In view of the truths which we have been considering, several practical lessons suggest themselves to our attention.

1. It becomes us to guard against those opinions and practices which tend to disparage the marriage institution or to impair a sense of its authority. In a corrupt state of society, infractions of the marriage law are treated with a kind of Parisian levity. Continence and chastity are made objects of ridicule; and even, if we may quote a phrase from the philosophic Hume, sneered at as "monkish virtues." This state of public sentiment is the sure precursor of national decay. Its progress may be slow and stealthy; but whensoever it shall have gained the ascendancy, the social organization will have become diseased to its very core. In the best days of ancient Rome, the marriage institution was invested with associations of sacredness and honor. From the building of the city, more than five centuries elapsed before there was recorded a single instance of DIVORCE. It seems that the example of Spurius Cabilius was morally contagious, so that at last, Cato, "the great moralist," resigned his wife to another man, who, at his death, made her his heir, and then her first husband received her as his own again. These licentious manners were in the full tide of triumph when those conquerors of

the world governed Judea, where King Herod took unto himself his brother Philip's wife, and then allowed John the Baptist to be beheaded for calling upon him to repent of his crime. Thus, throughout the realm of Roman civilization, the bonds of domestic life were thoroughly relaxed; and that relaxation was one of the mighty causes that contributed to that great event of modern history which it has tasked the genius of Gibbon to trace and delineate, the Decline and Fall of the Roman Empire.

Moreover, there are now abroad in the land various forms of Communism, wild socialistic theories, railing at the marriage law as a species of tyranny, decrying "the single family arrangements" as hostile to the spirit of genuine philanthropy or of universal love, and branding the household as "a den of selfishness." Such are the epithets of the celebrated Robert Owen, of Lanark, who spent his life in a vain attempt to promote general benevolence by extirpating private affections, and to remove vice and misery from the earth by laying it upon society to make full provision for the gratification of those constitutional desires which nature has implanted in the breast of every individual. As well might he have thought to make all men temperate by an ample supply of cold water, or to make all men wise by an equal distribution of books, as to make all men happy by a well-adjusted distribution of the elements of wealth. The evils to be remedied lie not so much in the physical condition as in the moral character of the men and women around us; and those principles and affections which constitute a sound and well-balanced character, are to be supplied, if at all, by the subtle, genial influences of home-life, rather than by the artificial apparatus of the Phalanstery. Mr. Owen, as we believe, was a sincere and kind-hearted man; so was Fourier, the most celebrated French Socialist; so, too, have been many others who have brought commanding talents and learning to the support of Communism. They have labored with a noble aim to remove some of the most terrible social evils that now afflict the masses of mankind. Nevertheless, their experiments have failed, and must fail until, in every scheme of social reörganization, they shall more clearly and fully recognize the obligations of the marriage law, the sacredness of the family, the permanence of the domestic relations, as well as the inalienable rights of the individual, in his personal relation to the civil government. Then, and not till then, will they be able to furnish a respectable share of contribution to the real progress of society; for every plan of reform which contravenes or overlooks the first principles of a simple New Testament Christianity, however splendid it may appear as an ideal theory, is destined at last to furnish a new practical commentary on that significant saying of Jesus: "Every plant which my heavenly Father has not planted shall be rooted up."

2. Since the marriage bond was ordained to form a

permanent union between the parties so long as they "both shall live," its obligations ought not to be assumed without that degree of *deliberation* which shall insure the full consent of the judgment and the heart. In what other event of earthly history is one's happiness more deeply involved? In what other event of earthly history is so much of playful recklessness exhibited? How many fix their destiny for life, as if it were all a matter of sport! Men jest about it even in their sage proverbs: they say, "Marriage is a lottery;" they say, "Matches are made in heaven;" thence they proceed to act, in regard to it, as if it were something that lies within the realm of Chance, or the realm of Fate, concerning which we poor mortals on the earth have no responsibility at all. What a spectacle of misery is there disclosed when two persons are joined together in the bonds of a sacred covenant without any previous consideration, without any congeniality of sentiment, or any kind of preparation for their common duties, toils, or cares! With both of them, perhaps, the project of such a union has sprung from a mere freak of fancy, from the impulse of a moment,—has been begun and carried through in the spirit of romance, while anticipation has invested the scenery of life with every tint and hue except those which are thrown over it by the experience of its realities. More than once have we seen the rash deed to have been followed by a long course of repentance. Yet even such a case is not hopeless. For more than once have I known that where the thoughtless, dashing young couple have committed such a mistake, and have become awakened to a sober sense of their condition, they have had the wisdom to make the best of it; so that, by mutual attentions, by forbearance, by acts of kindness, by a cultivated spirit of courtesy, those habits which are called a "second nature" have thriven by a gradual and healthy growth, and have laid a good foundation for domestic happiness. It was said, in a certain instance, that when the unfortunate victims of this sort of foolish rashness awoke from their dreamy illusion, that "each pitied the other, and pity was converted into love." Therefore let none despair; let it be the aim of the thoughtless pair to fulfil the duties enjoined by solemn vows, and the serene light of Heaven's smile may yet illumine their pathway. Especially, as we have seen, where the character of each of them has been modified by true religion, the effect has been wonderful; for gloom has given place to cheerfulness; the sounds of discord have died away, and the music of loving words has imparted to the hearth and home the aspect of a new creation. Nevertheless, although an antidote to the evil of rashness has sometimes been realized, let none on that account rush into solemn engagements thoughtlessly. In no act of human life should one more prayerfully seek the guidance of God. "Commit thy way unto Him, and He will direct thy paths." He will keep thee from fatal snares. Providence rules in behalf of those who feel their need of divine direction, and things that seem the most adverse to our wishes shall strangely work together for good to those who ask wisdom of Him. And when he deigns to bless the covenant which unites a couple in bonds that only death can sever, then shall be enjoyed the sweetness of domestic bliss, unmixed with drops of bitter, which neglect or temper sheds into its crystal cup.

3. The formation of the marriage union should always be prompted by genuine affection. The scriptural precept enjoins it upon the husband that he love his wife even as himself. If a man be conscious that he is incapable of cherishing towards the companion of his choice an affection of such purity, depth, and strength,—in that case, for him "it is not good to marry." The divine law is, too, that the wife should be subject to her husband; and if, while unmarried, she be not conscious of a love that would render obedience to this law practicable for her, it would be a perilous experiment for her to assume the marriage vow. For while nothing is more beautiful than the harmony of kindred hearts, nothing is more hateful than the constant chafing that comes from the forced companionship of those whose characters are unadjusted to each other.

There can be no compensation for the want of genial love in a married pair. Without it, the best means of enjoyment that wealth can furnish become insipid; even palatial grandeur is dreary, beauty is as "painted flame," courtesy itself seems as hollow mockery, and the heart sighs in vain for that sympathy which imparts a zest to prosperity, blunts the sting of calamity, and pours a renovating balm of life through every faculty of one's nature. Such marriage unions as calculating parents sometimes plan from mercenary motives, have been the bane and curse of many a family for successive generations. The springs of social life are poisoned by the moral malaria that hang murkily around the abodes of those who are the victims of such heartless schemes. For, although equality of rank, fortune, and position, may have its advantages, these are all lighter than the small dust of the balance when weighed against those qualities of *character* which form the basis of a real and permanent union.

If the great principles and the practical rules which have now been considered, could be effectually commended to the minds and hearts of a single generation so as to be realized in action, what an altered aspect would the social condition of our race exhibit! What a mighty stride would have been made towards the attainment of that state of millennial bliss which the Harp of Prophecy has for ages celebrated! How speedily would our globe be set throughout with happy homes! The hard lot of poverty would be softened, the deceptive glare of wealth and fashion would give place to the healthful sunlight of inward peace; and the earth, as it rolls in its orbit, if surveyed by the inhabitants of purer realms, would be hailed by them as a school of education, formed by the hand of the Almighty to rear a fallen race for honor, glory, and immortality. Thanks be to God that, despite the murmurs of discontent, the wails of woe, the ravages of sin, which beset us on every hand, there are *some homes* wherein these benign effects are enjoyed in their reality and fulness: let it be ours to do what in us lieth to render them the free, the transmitted heritage of our own and of every land.

Duties of the Husband.

"HUSBANDS, LOVE YOUR WIVES, AND BE NOT BITTER AGAINST THEM."—Colossians iii. 19.

A WELL-ORDERED family, presided over by a married couple who are united by sincere affection, by kindred sentiments, and by one general aim of life, is a lovely moral spectacle that is fitted to attract the sympathies of angels towards our fallen world. It is the genial nursery of all that is noble in human character; and when the spirit of pure religion rules in the breast of every member of it, there is seen a closer approximation to the society of heaven than can be found in any other earthly association. It is one of the finest products of Christianity, and one which has been known to attract the admiring gaze of a calm heathen observer with a power all its own. Scarcely any thing can be mentioned that carries with it a more marked contrast with every social aspect of Paganism. Hence, the fathers of our missionary enterprise, at the outset of their work, were desirous that those who went forth to teach Christianity to the idolatrous nations should be heads of families, in order that they might illustrate by example the dignity of woman, her right to equal companionship with man, the reality and the beauty of domestic virtue. That, however, which we would wish to present to the heathen as a just and favorable specimen of pure religion, we should cultivate amongst ourselves, not only that we may "adorn the doctrine of God in all things," but that we may enjoy the full possession of those social blessings which Christianity is designed to bestow.

In order to aid ourselves in doing so, let us consider some of the chief duties which spring from the marriage relation.

First, in the order of nature and of relative worth, is that habit of generous affection which the apostle enjoins in the precept, "Husbands, love your wives, and be not bitter against them."

With some persons it is a cherished opinion that it is of very little use to give forth any general rule touching the cultivation of mutual love: that if the conditions of spontaneous love exist in the natural character, then, where kindred spirits meet, it will thrive of itself; and that without this preparation for it, no art, no rules, or practised skill, can call it into being. This opinion contains a portion of truth. The elements of mutual attachment must undoubtedly be implanted in the heart by the God of nature; but then it is equally evident that when they are there, they may be blighted by neglect, or crushed beneath the heavy tramp of worldly cares and excited passions. Very truthful to nature, and a just observation of mankind, are the words of the Irish poet:

A something light as air—a look,
A word unkind or wrongly taken,
The love that tempests never shook,
A breath, a touch like this, has shaken;
And ruder winds will soon rush in
To spread the breach that words begin;
And eyes forget the gentle ray
They wore in Hymen's smiling day;
And voices lose the tone that shed
A tenderness round all they said;
Till fast declining, one by one,
The sweetnesses of love are gone;
And hearts, so lately mingled, seem
Like broken clouds, or like the stream
That smiling left the mountain's brow,
As though its waters ne'er could sever,
Yet ere it reach the plain below
Breaks into floods, and parts for ever.

It is not at all improbable that when the inspired writer of my text addressed the precept which it contains particularly to husbands, it was obvious to his view that they are more liable than the partners of their fortunes to become deficient in those things which strengthen true affection; more apt to assume the reproving look, the tone of dissatisfaction, thus bearing to their peaceful homes a little of that chafed temper which is often caused, amidst the strife of life, by hard contact with the selfish and designing, and which is almost sure to follow, for a little while at least, that rasping of one's sensibilities which is inevitable in the collisions of business. The man of active habits and of many cares, all-engrossed with the concerns of his own sphere, forgets sometimes the difficulties of managing a house, and the unrelaxing pressure that daily comes upon the weaker nerves of her to whom he looks for some balmy influence that shall soothe and cheer his own perturbed spirit. And then, a slight disappointment as to the arrangements for his comfort, either in regard to the punctual observance of his dining-hour or to the manner of preparing for it, or as to some omission that has caused a little jar in the machinery of the household, has been sufficient to cloud his brow with gloom, and to indicate a sense of provocation, even though no harsh word gave token of a ruffled mind. Now, in the hearts of this amiable couple there may have been a real, a joyous love; and when their lips pronounced the vows of the sacred covenant, each may have imagined the other to have been an angel; and if, at last, they should happen to discover that they are both imperfect human beings, let them guard against the shock incidental to a reäction of the feelings. Let them have a care against brooding over these little infelicities, and magnifying them beyond measure, so as to give place to a stealthy, mutual disesteem; but let them cherish at once a generous pity for each other's failures, griefs, or weaknesses, and a brave resolve to soften each other's lot in the spirit of their plighted faith. Especially let the husband, whose breast is most exposed to boisterous agitation and to the rough play of conflicting feelings, strive thoroughly to master his own spirit, so that he be not "bitter" against her whose worldly destiny is in his hands, and who is, therefore, most keenly sensible to the effect of every look, word, or tone that may seem to have an unkindly meaning.

And here, lest I should fail to mention it in another connection, I would fain whisper a word of counsel in the ear of the wife. If such a case as this just alluded to, or aught akin to it, should ever occur in your domestic history, do not allow a cool or warm retort to escape your lips, nor let your spirit sink in silent sullenness, but aim at once to bring the current of feeling back to its smooth and regular channels; then forget the past, and let the course of affairs move on as if its surface had not been rippled.

II. Another duty which the Scriptures enjoin upon the husband is this: that he make his own home—the home of his heart—in the house where his wife abides. Thus, an apostle says, "Ye husbands, DWELL with them according to knowledge." (1 Pet. iii. 7.) Paul seems to regard a compliance with this precept as a matter of course on the part of Christian men, when he directs the wife who wishes information on a religious subject, instead of calling for it in a promiscuous assembly, to converse respecting it with her husband at home. (1 Cor. xiv. 35.) All this involves the idea of intelligent and affectionate companionship. It implies a habit of instructive conversation. It implies, too, that the man who realizes the character of a good husband, according to the Christian conception of it, is not possessed of a restless, roving spirit, which disqualifies him for the enjoyment of an evening in the company of his wife or in the bosom of his family.

> "The first sure symptom of a mind in health,
> Is rest of heart and pleasure felt at home."

It ill agrees with the benign aims of the marriage

institution for a man to have a house, yet to be virtually, and of his own accord, a *non-resident.* Many an amiable woman, however, finds to her sorrow a marked contrast between the eagerness with which her society was sought before marriage and the readiness with which it is abandoned afterwards. If she be unconscious of any fault on her part, of any change in temper or deportment likely to alienate affection, a corroding grief will inevitably settle upon her spirits. It may be long concealed, but its stealthy ravages will be felt. Especially will it be so if haunts of idle dissipation are seen to affect his tastes, to charm him away from his once-loved hearth, and to be throwing their potent spells over his wavering mind. How can she resist the dread conviction that to a true home-love her husband is a stranger; that this finest, strongest bond of all the social affections is utterly wanting? The real mental bliss of domestic life he enjoys not; and the estrangement of his feelings from their proper centre was aptly expressed by a French nobleman who was accustomed to visit every evening the mansion of an accomplished widow, the Countess of Rochefort, in order to enjoy her society. As he had been deprived of his wife by death, it was suggested by one of his friends that it would be well for him to become united to the Countess by marriage. "I have often thought so," he replied; "but one thing prevents me. In that case, where should I spend my evenings?" "Many a truth is spoken in jest;" but this man, doubtless, expressed his sense of a serious difficulty, by no means rarely felt in the beautiful land of his nativity, which displays such an abundance of gayety without contentment, of gratification without happiness, of habitations without homes.

What though it be true that the demands of business, and numerous occasions which we need not name or classify, will often call one away from the society of his own family? When these calls are yielded to as *cases of necessity*, they may be attended with incidental benefits. For then, instead of fostering tastes adverse to the enjoyments of the family circle, they will aid in strengthening the domestic affections, and will incline the heart to welcome the tranquil pleasures of home-life with a quickened zest. Not so, however, when *absenteeism* (to use a word now common in England) becomes a matter of choice. The bonds of sympathy are then gradually relaxed; the affections cease to play around their proper centre; the force of habit daily increases the estrangement, and the uneasiness of a homeless heart verifies the proverb, "As a bird that wandereth from her nest, so is a man that wandereth from his place."

III. Still further, the Christian law renders it obligatory on the husband that he cherish towards his wife the sentiment of *honor*. This duty is enjoined by the expressive sentence, "giving honor unto the wife as the weaker vessel." (1 Pet. iii. 7.) The command implies that the wife sustains to the husband not only a relation of endearment, but also of *dignity*. The tribute of honor which it claims for her cannot always be rendered merely by kind words and affectionate manners. It includes also, as a general rule, what is commonly called "an honorable maintenance or support." As she is by nature of weaker frame, as her sensibilities are more lively, her secluded sphere of duties sufficiently engrossing, it devolves upon the husband to procure, if need be, by the strength of his arm and the sweat of his brow, the means of an honorable livelihood. "For, if a man provide not for his own," says Paul, "especially for those of his own household, he hath denied the faith, and is worse than an infidel." In barbarous countries, and throughout the whole realm of paganism, both the law and the custom are very different. There, the life of the man is one of lordly and capricious ease, while the life of the woman is one of toil and slavery. She is either doomed to hard labor, or kept and decorated as the toy of leisure and amusement. She may be petted and caressed; her vanity may be flattered, and every passion may be gratified, but she is seldom *honored*. Like Vashti, the beautiful Queen of Persia, whose exaltation and disgrace are so vividly depicted in the book of Esther, every wife may be forced to feel that her happiness is the sport of caprice, and that her fate for this world hangs on the whim of a fitful master. But Christianity exalts woman to a nobler sphere, reveals the dignity of her immortal nature, declares with a voice of authority in the ear of man, "She is thy companion, the wife of thy covenant," and claims for her the tribute of honor which is due to the moral grandeur of her mission.

In fulfilling the precept which requires the husband to give honor to the wife, in no respect is he under more solemn obligation than he is to honor her *conscience*, and to allow her, as an *inalienable right*, full liberty to carry out practically her religious convictions. For conscience is God's vicegerent in the soul, and speaks, when it speaks at all, with the tone of supreme authority. When the mind of a sensitive woman recognizes its voice and is impelled to some some act of obedience, perhaps by making a profession of religion, or else by discharging some other sacred obligation, how pitiable must be her condition if he, whose approving smile, next to the favor of God alone, is her chief earthly joy, place himself in an attitude of resistance athwart her pathway! How stern and racking the conflict of her feelings! The first coming of such a trial is a great era of her moral history. There is only one right course for her to take; she must "obey God rather than man:" and this, if truly enlightened, she will do with a self-sacrificing, heroic spirit, well knowing that the calm sunlight of a good conscience is worth more than all the wealth of empires,—yea, worth more than all the treasures of the most favored earthly home. Complicate and difficult, however, does such a case become, if it happen that, through partial ignorance or a blind fanaticism, she has been led to neglect the duties which she owes to her husband and her home, under the plea of religion; for then the sentiment of right becomes his strong support, even though he push his demands to the last extremity. But if she be blessed with an ordinary share of woman's wit and common sense, in connection with a high-souled conscientiousness, she will be susceptible of those remedial influences that flow from the teachings of the Scriptures, which always regard the duties relating to the family as really a part of Christianity as those which are performed in the devotional circle or in the public sanctuary. Nevertheless, in this line of direction, so many men of all ranks of society are disposed to act the tyrant, that in the marriage ceremony I cannot use the word "obey," in the woman's pledge to the partner of her life, except as connected with the qualifying phrase, "in all lawful things;" because it is never to be forgotten that, far above all domestic, civil, and social law, the higher law of God stands forth, laying its obligations on every rational soul, in its own separate individuality,—"the law of laws," invested with the sanctions of eternal majesty, and uttering its commands in the name of the Supreme Authority of the universe.

Moreover, in honoring the wife the husband should see to it that he fitly honor the finer feelings of her nature. The scenes of common life furnish ample proofs that this hint is not superfluous; so many there are who err in allowing too little to the discretion of the wife. They treat her like a child. They seem to deprive themselves of that element of domestic happiness brought to view in Solomon's fine picture of a virtuous woman, of whom he says, "The heart of her hnsband doth safely trust in her, so that he shall have no need of spoil." They deal out their money with such a pitiful nicety, that she cannot give a cent to any object of benevolence in which she may be interested, without asking her husband's opinion, or making it a matter of grave discussion. In such a case as this, a man does not treat his wife as an equal; he does not *honor* her with his confidence. He places her in a state of bondage, at war with confiding love and a proper self-respect. Of course, if there be an inability on his part to meet the promptings of a generous nature, she should be the first to know it, and the last to expect him to do so. But on this point, the one may misjudge as well as the other; and, as a general rule, we may safely say that a man honors himself in paying a tribute of honor to the judgment of his wife. We have never known this more beautifully illustrated than it was in the example of a distinguished gentleman who was unhappily indifferent to the things of religion and to all benevolent enterprises, but whose wife, an excellent Christian lady, was cordially engaged in promoting them. This wealthy merchant was applied to by a clergyman for a donation to a Missionary Society. He refused to comply with the request. He urged various objections, but concluded by saying, "You may call on my wife; perhaps she will take a different view of the subject; and if so, will act according to her pleasure." In relating this incident, the clergyman observed, "I stood mute with astonishment for a moment or two. I said within myself, This man *ought* to be a Christian, for he has a soul gifted by nature with all the *material* that is needful to form a noble Christian, if it were only sanctified and refined by the grace of God."

And while I urge on the conscience and heart of the husband this precept of Christianity, bidding him to cherish towards his wife the sentiment of honor, I may be allowed to remark that Christianity speaks on this point with special emphasis, inasmuch as it is her peculiar mission to exalt woman to that position in society where her influence may be universally felt in promoting the happiness of the race. Situated as most of us have been, in a Christian country, we can but feebly conceive of a state of society over which woman exerts no humanizing influence whatever, in which she has no rights, and in which, by becoming either the toy or slave of man, she is made to minister to his debasement rather than his elevation. In no instance, perhaps, is the evil effect of man's apostasy upon the relations of this world more apparent than in this, wherein, as Milton would express it,

> ——— disproportion'd Sin
> Jarred against Nature's chime,

and marred the moral and social harmonies of creation. Take away from our social state the bland, softening, and conservative influence of woman, and what is there left? A wild chaos of brutal appetites and disordered passions; a condition worse than that of savage life,—because the refinements of civilization would but inflame the lowest propensities without furnishing any counterpoise to their excess, or any principle to regulate them.

IV. Last of all, though this consideration be not the least of all, let it be remembered that the husband is bound by the divine law to treat his wife as an immortal being, and, therefore, to have regard to her moral and spiritual welfare. In those nations of the earth which form the broad realm of heathenism, and which are so deeply cursed by female degradation, it is very evident that this miserable state of things is chiefly the effect of a superstition which has practically banished from the common mind the idea of an immortal nature as the Creator's gift to woman, imparting to her a moral dignity that transcends all earthly relations. Although the Koran of Mahomet holds forth the rewards of Paradise to both sexes, yet his conceptions of the future world were so sensual, low, and mean, that the common belief in its existence furnishes no moral incentives adapted to work out the proper elevation of woman in the social life of the present world. Not so "the law of Christ." That exalts domestic life by shedding around it the light of immortality. It requires that the husband and the wife should dwell together "as heirs of the grace of life," and declares that in that state of "glory yet to be revealed," although the marriage covenant shall have been dissolved, faithful women shall vie in moral beauty with beings that have never known sin; that they shall be "even as the angels." Can any man have a just sense of the truth that the partner of his heart, the sharer of his fortunes, whose earthly destiny is so closely linked with his own, is, like himself, an immortal spirit; that, after the scenes of time shall all have vanished from her view like a gorgeous dream, she must enter upon those brighter ones that shall be for ever expanding in beatific splendor, or else, if unprepared for them, must dwell in those gloomy realms which our Saviour describes as "the outer darkness" of banishment from God and happiness, and yet cherish no lively interest in her education for the society of heaven? In that remarkable hour that witnessed the formation of the marriage-union, the era of separation was anticipated by the solemn vow which his lips then uttered, that he would cherish the object of his choice as "the wife of his covenant" in wedded love "till death should part them." And say, I pray you, can any true-hearted man thus give his hand to one of kindred soul, to be the companion of his pilgrimage onward to the verge of death's dark valley, and yet have no thought or care as to her preparation to pass serenely through that place of terrors whither she must go *alone*, so that even amidst its chill ing shadows she may greet with joy the glorious destiuation towhich Heaven beckons her, to which her God invites her aspirations and her faith? O no! To be indifferent to interests so momentous, he must be destitute of all the higher elements of humanity, and deaf to all the voices which speak with solemn eloquence to every listening ear from the heights and depths of the spiritual universe.

Most aptly illustrative of that aspect of moral sublimity with which a simple religious faith invests the scene of separation that must come in due time to every wedded pair, is Cotton Mather's description of the trial of his own heart when the pall of gloom enshrouded his abode. Hear his plaintive wail while it dies away into a strain of heavenly music: "The black day arrives. I had never seen so black a day in all the time of my pilgrimage. The desire of my eyes is this day to be taken from me at a stroke. Her death is lingering and painful. All the forenoon of this day she was in the pangs of death, and sensible till the last minute or two before her final expiration. I cannot remember the discourse that passed between us; only her devout soul was full of satisfaction about her going to a state of blessedness with the Lord Jesus Christ. As far as my distress would permit, I studied to confirm her satisfaction and consolation. When I saw to what a point of resignation I was called of the Lord, I resolved with his help to glorify him. So, two hours before she expired, I kneeled by her bedside, and took into my hands that dear hand, the dearest in the world, and solemnly and sincerely gave her up to the Lord. I gently put her out of my hands, and laid away her hand, resolved that I would not touch it again. She afterwards told me that she signed and sealed my act of resignation; and though before that she had called for me continually, *after* it, she never asked for me any more. She conversed much until near two in the afternoon. The last sensible word that she spoke was to her weeping father — 'Heaven, heaven, will make amends for all.'" Ah, what a touching spectacle was this! Did poetry ever celebrate a scene more radiant with the glow of moral heroism than that which is depicted in this plain narrative, which exhibits a frail woman amidst the agonies of dissolution hailing her immortality, while the chamber of death becomes to her the portal of Paradise?

And yet, it may be that some kind and sympathetic husband who is listening to me now may feel conscious while I speak of such an utter want of that deep mental peace inspired by Christian faith as quite disqualifies him to meet in a becoming manner an emergency like this. If so, then admit, I entreat you, with manly candor, your imperative and immediate need of the religion of the gospel in order to be prepared aright for the relations and duties of life. Seek this first of all. Seek it now. The boon of Christ's kingly grace awaits your acceptance. You may neglect and reject it; and without it there may be much of earthly enjoyment in the domestic relations; but how sad is the thought that it must all so soon and sadly end! Behold, then, "the one thing needful;" the crowning qualification for the real, the enduring happiness of home-life. Make it thine own; let it be "thy chosen heritage." Then, indeed, death may break the marriage covenant, but cannot part the happy pair; for what God hath thus "joined together," neither time, nor change, nor prosperity, nor adversity, nor sickness, nor death can ever "put asunder."

Duties of the Wife.

"LET THE WIFE SEE THAT SHE REVERENCE HER HUSBAND."
Ephesians v. 33.

THERE is much of practical wisdom expressed in the homely Irish proverb, "a man must ask his wife's leave to be rich." The saying is verified by common experience. And not only so, but experience proves that the proverb which asserts a man's dependence on his wife for the acquisition of wealth might justly take a wider scope, and declare, without reserve, his dependence on her for his happiness in all the walks of life. We may easily imagine him to be the owner of untold wealth, and that wealth to be as firmly secured as possible against every hazard; we may picture him forth to the eye of fancy as having at his command all the means of gratification that art, science, and a refined civilization can afford; but if the partner of his fortunes be unfitted for her proper sphere, if she have no heart for its employments, if her taste and her temper be uncongenial with the unobtrusive virtues that are the essential elements of a peaceful home, his fine advantages will but enhance his misery, and render the pangs of disappointment that vibrate through his breast more subtle and more poignant.

With this truth in view, there seems to be but little likelihood of our placing too high an estimate on the importance of the subject that now lies before us; and while I proceed to exhibit the duties of woman in the relation of the wife, I will follow chiefly, in the selection of topics, the suggestions of the Sacred Scripture; a Book which reveals a religion adapted to the scenes of every-day life, and throws around us its incentives, lights, and aids to happiness in all our ordinary walks, as well as in the great emergencies of this mortal state.

The first duty, then, which I commend to the attention of the wife, is correlative with that which I have urged, first of all, on the regard of the husband: that which Paul commanded Titus to inculcate on the young wife of his time, namely, that *she love her husband.* The expression implies that sincere affection is to be made a subject of careful cultivation. This precept has fallen on the ears of many who, for the want of experience or reflection, do not discern its point or force. They speak of love as being so spontaneous in its nature that whensoever it hath scope it will inhale new life from its own freedom, and, therefore, regard any precept touching its culture as quite superfluous. They significantly inquire, Can moral, artistic, or religious rules produce real love? But the aim of the precept is not to produce the affection, but rather to guard against those inadvertences which so often paralyze it; to anticipate the stealthy influence of those foibles or infirmities which check its growth; to rouse the mind

4*

to prepare itself for those adverse incidents which sometimes take the most affectionate couple by surprise, and which, rising suddenly like a dark thunder-cloud over a lovely summer's sky, change the whole aspect of that little world which we at once dignify and endear when we designate it as our home. In the majority of cases where strong mutual attachment has been followed by coldness, indifference or aversion, the change has not been brought about by the shock of some great event, by the blast of misfortune or the persecution of enemies. These unite more firmly than ever hearts which are susceptible of genuine affection; a truth finely commemorated by Irving in his Sketch-Book, where his lifelike picture of "The Wife" in scenes of adversity, so beautifully illustrates that poetical saying with which he has graced his page:

> **The treasures of the deep are not so precious**
> **As are the concealed comforts of a man**
> **Locked up in woman's love.**

"There is in every true woman's heart a spark ot heavenly fire, which lies dormant in the broad daylight of prosperity; but which kindles up, and beams, and blazes, in the dark hour of adversity." The companions of a journey cling to each other with courageous sympathy, when called to breast the storm together. But while they move with somewhat weary steps along life's dusty pathway, engaged, perhaps, in a jading routine of daily duties, then latent perils lurk around them. A hasty word followed by a rough or keen retort a disappointment about some trifling thing, an appearance of neglect produced by concealed yet corroding care, a want of sympathetic consideration in those petty trials and annoyances which are rarely understood if not personally felt;—these are the things which wear harder on the ties of attachment than the severest shock of outward calamity. Many and touching cases could I recount wherein a wife has received intelligence of a terrible reverse in her husband's fortunes without a murmur, wherein the blow that smote their budding hopes developed the character of each in nobler proportions, in beauty, strength, and grandeur; but I could speak, too, of instances in which the heart of the wife was at first pained, then almost alienated or paralyzed by perceiving that her husband could not apprehend her difficulties, and that he expected more of her than she could accomplish. If, in the management of the house, there were any interruption of order or punctuality, any failure to meet his plans and wishes, there was, on his part, not only the feeling of disappointment, but also the look or tone of censure, and some sort of intimation that if he had nothing more to do than to take care of a household, he could easily make the course of things run smoothly, and have much leisure on his hands. A careless remark like this has sometimes roiled the springs of feeling more deeply, and called forth tears more bitter than the most sweeping blast of adversity could have done. Once I knew a thriving, wealthy man, who deemed himself to be highly gifted with a talent for management and economy, whose criticisms of this nature distilled a fatal blight upon an early love that had seemed sincere and strong. I never doubted that their love, at first, was real. But she was unprepared for the trials which it was destined to meet. The first expression that jarred against its harmonies was unexpected. She allowed it to have a more weighty effect upon her spirits than it deserved, and magnified it by poring over it in solitude. Her brow was clouded when it might as well have been serene. In any case like this, it becomes the wife, and especially the young and inexperienced one, to remember that it rarely happens that even the most thoughtful person can acquire a just conception of another's difficulties without having been placed in a similar situation; that much is to be attributed to her husband's want of thought or knowledge, rather than want of affection; and that, therefore, she must not allow the suspicion of alienated feeling to prey upon her agitated mind. If indulged at all, it will consume her peace, although her manners be unaltered; just as the rose which seems so fair without, enwraps the worm that wastes its core. Let her, at the very outset of married life, be aware of the sober truth which Cowper has so well expressed:

> "The kindest and the happiest pair
> Will find occasion to forbear,
> And something every day they live
> To pity, and, perhaps, forgive."

Therefore, let her guard against a decline of affection by resolving to overlook and forget these little interruptions of harmony, to command her own spirit, and to keep her heart strong in the exercise of her early love, in spite of them.

The fitness of this precept, which I have quoted and interpreted, to strengthen by careful culture the principle of love, must, then, be obvious to us all. In the days of early acquaintanceship, before marriage, a couple, conscious of spontaneous and mutual attachment, and enjoying each other's society, may imagine that their love is unsusceptible of any serious shock; that it can afford to laugh at cautious counsels, and set every storm at defiance. Well, this is a delightful sentiment. I would not dispel it by needless alarms. I would only have the eyes of both open to their liability to perils that have too often proved real, so that they may be prepared to escape them. Let it not be forgotten that in days of courtship character is not thoroughly tried, and that in other circumstances it may be transformed. It is very agreeable for a gentleman in an evening hour, free from care, to meet the lady whom he esteems, to enjoy her conversation, to listen to her strains of music, or participate with her in some social entertainment, but it is quite another thing to be her daily associate when new responsibilities and new cares thoroughly try her intellect and nerves, her fortitude and wisdom; and that, too, when the rasping collisions of an exciting business put severely to the test his own powers of endurance and self-possession. The vessel newly launched and lying at anchor in the smooth waters of the harbor may attract admiration for the beauty of her proportions, the excellence of her trim, and the grace with which she reposes on the glassy surface of the bay; but when, with all sails set, having left her port, she encounters the winds and surges of the deep, then comes the searching test of her character, and not till then are her weak points, if any there be, clearly brought to view. In anticipation of such a trial, it is always wise and safe to give due care to the strengthening of every part, setting an extra beam here, and a brace there, where a failure may be feared.

2. Hence, let me proceed to observe that it becomes a wife habitually to cherish what the Scriptures designate "a meek and quiet spirit." Well does the Apostle Peter praise it as the true ornament of woman; for nothing so adorns her character in the eyes of men, and in the sight of God it "is of great price." Nothing invests her with such an all-conquering power; and without this, even though she may get, she cannot *keep* in her hand that moral sceptre which it should be her pride and joy to wield at home. Without gentleness of soul and manner a mother cannot rule a child; much less can a wife properly influence a husband. More than she may be aware is she the light and attraction of his home; and if from her he anticipate, on his entrance there, peevishness, instead of cheerfulness, the reproving look instead of the smile of welcome, opposition instead of acquiescence in his wishes, the charm is broken; and in him there is strengthened, almost unconsciously, perhaps, the tendency to linger on his way thither, and to leave it for some "engagement" as soon as he can. There is nothing wonderful in this, for it is a truth which was penned many centuries ago, that "it is better to dwell in the wilderness than with a contentious and angry

woman," or on "the corner of the house-top than with a scolding woman" in a spacious mansion. Pride or contentiousness is no ornament to a *man*, but it is a greater deformity to a woman; yet, in spite of her gentler nature, it will sometimes rule in her breast; a fact expressed in the mythology of the Greeks as prominently as it is in our Bible, for they represented not only the GRACES as female figures, but the FURIES also.

How aptly, then, has Hannah More touched the springs of domestic happiness in sober verse:

> "The angry look suppressed, the taunting thoughts;
> Subduing and subdued the petty strife
> Which clouds the color of domestic life;
> The sober comfort, all the peace which springs
> From the large aggregate of little things;
> On these small cares of daughter, wife, or friend,
> The almost sacred joys of home depend."

3. But besides all this, the Scriptures enjoin it upon the wife to "see that she *reverence* her husband." This duty is the correlative of that which is enjoined upon the husband by the precept that bids him to *honor* his wife. The sentiment of reverence is to be cherished on her part, not merely when it may be called forth by his character as a man, but in view of the *relation* formed by the marriage covenant. Wheresoever it is genuine, it will be made manifest not only on special occasions, and in her general deportment, but it will express itself also in her *words*. And when we speak of words, we do not mean merely what

may be designated by letters and syllables, but also by enunciation and tone. The injunction forbids that sort of pertness with which some have been known to talk about a husband, or, as it has been expressed, to "talk at him;" a habitude which is inconsistent with the respect due to the conjugal relation, however often a man's faults may present fair marks for wit or satire. I remember once to have been sadly shocked on observing a husband make his own wife the subject of ridicule in company. Nor was I less disturbed, in another instance, on beholding the unnatural sight of a wife, distinguished among her sex for the gift of speech, emblazoning the foibles of her husband with a conversational eloquence worthy of a better theme. "There is that speaketh like the piercing of a sword, but the tongue of the wise is health."

But the reverence enjoined in the Sacred Scriptures relates to *conduct* as well as to words. Christianity found woman universally degraded in the social scale, and exalted her to a dignified and blest companionship with man, teaching us that in God's creation of the first pair, she was taken, not from his head, as if to be superior to him, nor from his feet, to be beneath him, but from his side, to be his equal, a friend and partner in all the cares and joys of life and love. But if at any time, unfortunately, there should be a difference of opinion or conflict of purpose on matters that require a choice of measures or courses of action, the authority and the responsibility of decision are vested in the husband. The exigences of life demand that such authority should exist *somewhere*, and unto him the

Almighty committed it originally, commanding the wife to be "subject in all things." Keenly searching indeed is the trial of character if the difficulty arise from ignorance or unreasonableness on his part; but then, in such a case, O thou more highly-gifted and favored woman, remember that thou art the wife of his covenant in plighted faith; and it is better, therefore, to bear the incidental evils of submission with heroic constancy, rather than abjure thy sacred vows, or rend asunder the bonds of thy obligation. These grievous things are an appointed part of thy probation on the earth; they form a fiery crucible of character, fitted to reveal its elements in those aspects of enduring beauty, purity, and worth, which command sincere and universal homage.

To this obligation of submission on the part of the wife, whensoever a difference of judgment unhappily occurs, there is one important case of exception. It is when conscience speaks as with the voice of God, and urges, in his name, and by his clearly revealed authority, the performance of a moral or religious duty. "All souls are his." Within the domain of morality and religion there is but one Sovereign, and it is at the eternal peril of any accountable being to admit the supremacy of another. In the person of Christ the Divinity was "made flesh, and dwelt among us;" and his word addresses itself to the heart and conscience of every man and of every woman, personally and individually, brooking the intervention of no superior authority on the part of man or angel, parent or friend, husband or priest. He speaks with the voice of adorable Majesty, and says to each and every one, The word that I have spoken, the same shall judge thee at the last day. Whoso loveth father or mother, or his own life, more than me, is not worthy of me." But where the dictates of religion, the voice of conscience and of God, demand a course of action on the part of a wife to which the husband does not give assent, her ready and cheerful submission to him in every other sphere should prove that it is the spirit of true religion alone, not self-will, captiousness, or caprice, which rules in her breast, supports her resolution, and determines her conduct.

And let it be remembered that the real dignity of such a motive of action the most irreligious men can appreciate and laud. The worth of religious principle as the basis of character in woman has been often acknowledged by those who are very far from practically admitting its supremacy over themselves. The developments of human nature which they have seen in the circles of fashion, as well as in other walks of life, have clearly shown to them that no other principle can furnish adequate security for the culture of those domestic virtues without which the conjugal relation is bereft of its charm, home of its sacredness, and the heart of its peaceful trust.

4. This leads me to observe that the Scriptures inculcate it as the duty of the wife to make it her aim to *please* her husband in all things—that is, in all things wherein compliance is not sinful. Paul says that the married man seeketh how to please his wife; he assumes that where there is a right spirit, this disposition prevails

as a matter of course. He also takes it for granted that the wife *seeketh how to please her husband.* This view of the subject stretches beyond the limit of definite rules, and gives to the mind and heart of each free play in studying how to promote the other's happiness. Love is inventive. Little attentions, unsought and unexpected, work mightily the permanent union of kindred minds. Their power to soothe and cheer, to cast a bland light over the roughnesses of life, is incalculable. Especially is this effect realized when they often occur at home. A pitiable contrast is sometimes displayed when those who are very affectionate and polite in their manners towards each other while abroad, are sullen, careless, or neglectful at home. Nevertheless, let the wife beware lest she cherish a jealousy as to her husband's personal attentions. What are they worth unless they are free? Then leave him to be free—to act himself, without being *teased* for attentions. And yet so winningly may you draw him, that he will follow at your beck, and every thing reasonable will be graceful and spontaneous. A man's spirit is in a state of constraint and slavery if he be forced to feel that the eye even of his wife follows him with a jealous scrutiny, and that she indulges repining and complaint because she cannot constantly engross him. Chiding words have sometimes fallen from woman's lips because a husband has gone forth on a ride, or a walk, or a journey, or has yielded himself to some social engagement, without due consultation with her, or without soliciting her company. But all cases of obligation have their natural limits, which should be observed.

If the Creator had intended no more mutual freedom than some seem to allow, couples might almost as well have been linked by nature, like the Siamese twins. The true moral affinity that unites a happy pair, requires the atmosphere of freedom; and while they are, in an interesting and sacred sense, ONE, their wills are free, their natural tastes remain, and therefore each should study how to please the other in all things.

This rule evidently extends to the most trifling things relating to home-life; to dress, carriage, manner, appearance; and all these should be regarded after marriage with as much care as they usually are before it. Human nature remains the same, and is pleased or displeased with the same things. It applies, too, to that oversight of the house, that presidency over the family circle which is necessary to secure there that order and regularity which will make it a desired and peaceful home. It is to be regretted that so many young ladies in our times are content with a fashionable boarding-school education, which is never sufficient to qualify any one for this honorable position. Even though it should be very good, *as far as it goes*, it needs to be followed by a faithful mother's tuition, and that constant training at home, whereby are imparted the practised eye and the fine tact which prepare one to make her house a scene of comfort, the abode of order, peace, and happiness.

Moreover, in seeking to please her husband, it should be the aim of a laudable ambition on the part of the wife, that he should have good reason, in the ultimate retrospect of their earthly course, to acknowledge with pleasure and gratitude her benign influence upon his mind and heart, his sentiments, his interests, and his whole character. One of the finest tributes in the English language to a woman's moral power, is from the pen of Sir James Mackintosh, who freely confesses that he was indebted to his wife for all his success as a scholar, as a civilian, as a public man; for all that rendered the memory of his career a source of pleasure; that it was she who roused him from inactivity, encouraged him in moments of despondency, soothed his irritability, and cheered him on to the pursuit of worthy aims with unfaltering purpose. If a man of so lofty a position and of such splendid acquisitions could furnish this explanation of his success, who shall say what bounds can be set to the moral influence of a wedded woman upon the man whose heart she sways by means of intelligence and love?

But in order to attain so high an end as this, the wife must qualify herself for conversational intercourse on subjects congenial with his tastes; on subjects that shall seem worthy of his regard in hours of retirement and in his graver moods of mind. For a task like this, the woman who is the mere devotee of fashion, whose thoughts are all engrossed with its glitter, its parade, and its trifling vanities, can have no power or fitness whatsoever. The idolatry of fashion dwarfs the intellect. It debases the heart. It renders the routine of life a scene of decorated meanness. Every man of sense, however worldly he may be, feels this, at times, in the very depths of his soul; and hence, will be apt to sympathize with the spirit of the appeal from the pen of a celebrated writer (a late member of the English Parliament, Henry Lytton Bulwer, in his work on France) against the mentally degrading influence of fashionable city-life. For, says he, "How is it possible that an Englishwoman—such as we ordinarily find the Englishwoman of London society—how is it possible that such a woman should possess the slightest influence over a man three degrees removed from dandyism and the Guards? What are her objects of interest but the most trumpery and insignificant? What are her topics of conversation but the most ridiculous and insipid? Not only does she lower down her mind to the emptiest-pated of the male creatures that she meets, but she actually persuades herself that it is charming and feminine to do so. She will talk to you about hunting and shooting—that is not unfeminine! Oh, no! But politics, the higher paths of literature, the stir and action of life in which all men worth any thing and from whom she could borrow any influence are plunged—of these she knows nothing, thinks nothing—in these she is not interested at all, and only wonders that an intellectual being can have any other ambition than to get what she calls good invitations to the stupidest, and hottest, and dullest of the stupid, hot, and dull drawing-rooms of London. There are, of course, reasons for all this; and I agree with a late work in asserting one of these reasons to be the practice which all England insists upon as so innocent, so virtuous, so modest, so disinterested; namely, "bringing out"—as it is called—a young woman at sixteen, who is ushered into a vast variety of crowded rooms with this injunction: 'There! go, hunt about and get a good' (which means a rich) 'husband.' Of late years this misfortune has been increasing, because fortune and rank are more entirely separated from talent and education; so that no man, after his reason has burst its leading-strings, ever now exposes himself to the insufferable *ennui* of general society." These remarks, as to their main bearing and significance, are worthy of regard on account of the source from which they come, having an impress of candor which they could not have shown so well had they proceeded from a French or American author. They indicate to every Christian reader how much the social life of the nineteenth century, even in its higher spheres of rank and wealth, need the refining influence of true Christianity, so happily adapted to calm its excitements, to regulate its passions, and elevate its aims. They indicate, too, to every thinking woman, where lies the secret of her moral strength. They suggest also, what kind of self-culture it becomes her to seek if she would truly *please*, and in pleasing, exert an enduring influence over a manly mind, so as to command sincere esteem and fulfil her beneficent mission in the world.

5. Still further, let it be remembered that it is the duty of the wife to promote, as far as may be in her power, tne *religious welfare* of her husband. However eligible may be the worldly condition of any couple, however congenial their natural tastes and sentiments, their happiness is very far from being complete, if, as spiritual and immortal beings, they are destitute of that "lively hope" of an "unfading inheritance," so much

spoken of in the Scriptures, which flings its light across the vale of Death, and irradiates the prospect of eternity. Can they be happy, when the very thought of separation at the grave is regarded only as a hostile intruder, whose presence is unrelieved by any well-founded expectation of a reünion in a higher state of being? Will it not visit them unbidden? Will it not cast a pall of gloom over the most brilliant scenes, and dispel the enchantments of pleasure? Undoubtedly. Unless they can aid each other onward in the path to heaven, "dwelling together as heirs of the grace of life," their mutual happiness in its best estate is but superficial, and destined soon to perish like the gorgeous scenery of a dream. And therefore, the question which came of old, from the pen of an apostle, sounds out an appeal that is fitted to thrill the sensibilities of every true-hearted woman who has assumed the vows of the marriage-covenant: "How knowest thou, O wife, but thou mayest save thy husband?"

Ponder well the meaning of that appeal. As if it had fallen upon thine ear directly from the skies, as if it had come from the lips of an angel flashing celestial splendors around him. O thou highly favored, Christian wife, open thy heart to its weighty import. Let the eternal welfare of thy husband be an object of chief regard. Seek it with unfaltering constancy. Be not easily discouraged. In the pursuit of such an aim there can be no compensation for the evil of failure, and success will be worth more than the treasures of a thousand worlds. If this end shall have been attained, then, when Death shall part you, it will be with the joyous anticipation of meeting in that glorious realm where, though there be "no marrying or giving in marriage," heart is knit to heart, and kindred spirits mingle in the harmonies of pure, perfect, and immortal friendship. Then may be applied to domestic love what the poet of Hope has said of his favorite theme:

> When yonder spheres sublime
> Pealed their first notes to sound the march of Time,
> Thy joyous youth began; yet not to fade
> When all the sister-planets have decayed;
> When wrapt in fire the realms of ether glow,
> And Heaven's last thunders shake the world below,
> Thou shalt in triumph o'er the ruins smile,
> And light thy torch at Nature's funeral-pile.

Duties of Parents to Children.

"TRAIN UP A CHILD IN THE WAY HE SHOULD GO, AND WHEN HE IS OLD HE WILL NOT DEPART FROM IT."—Proverbs xxii. 6.

WHAT a memorable era in the history of a married couple is the commencement of the parental relation! It is not easy at a single glance fully to apprehend its importance. The event is generally a theme of congratulation in the domestic circle, and among the friends of the family the infant stranger is hailed with a sympathetic welcome. When the first mother gazed upon the first child, her heart was full of wonder and joy; she pressed it to her bosom as a heaven-sent gift, and, xclaiming, "I have gotten a man from the Lord," she named him Cain, a word which expresses the idea of an *acquisition*. But she little thought of the acquisition of cares and troubles for herself that were enfolded in the fortunes of that boy, of the elements of evil that were to gain strength by every throb of that infantile heart, which seemed to beat in answer to her own. Fearful was the contrast between the time of childhood, when she could so naturally indulge the thought that he had been given to his parents in order to beguile them of their wearying toils by his laughing mirth, his freaks of sportive innocence, and that dark day when he imbrued his hands in a younger brother's blood! When we gaze at first upon the winning features of a little child, we are disposed, like Eve, to predict for it a happy destiny; but sage experience chastens our glowing fancies by teaching us that the complexion of that destiny must depend on the character that shall be formed in youth, and that must be formed, too, for the most part, under a parent's eye and influence.

Fond parent, Father! Mother! now engaged from day to day in watching over the growth and progress of your little one, and luxuriating in glad anticipations of the time when that child shall walk before you in all the pride and strength of early manhood, or in all the charms of accomplished womanhood; say truly whether or not you have pondered well the weighty trust committed to you? If there had been devolved on you by some royal grant the care of educating one who was by birth and blood heir to the throne of an extensive empire, what words could measure your sense of obligation touching the duty of preparing him for that station of power and peril, of dignity and splendor? Nevertheless, how low and narrow is a place like that, of a few years' duration, compared with the boundless sphere to be occupied by the spirit of the infant now sleeping in its cradle, when, having conquered Sin and Death, it shall soar like a seraph among "the sons of light" on high, or else, the victim of depraved passions, and "led captive' by the Arch-tempter, he shall go "to his own place" with kindred spirits, among the fallen and the lost!

In view of a responsibility so momentous and thrilling, the saying which forms my text is full of incitement and comfort; full of incitement to action, because it exhibits definitely and in few words the great duty of a parent; and full of comfort, because it declares the moral certainty of a happy result whensoever that duty is faithfully performed.

Let us consider, then,

I. What is here proposed as the great thing to be done.

II. The points to be regarded in the doing of it.

"Train up a child in the way he should go," is the concise and comprehensive precept wherein divine wisdom announces the chief duty of a parent. The boldness and strength of expression with which the effect of a faithful training up of a child is here affirmed, have been the occasion of perplexity to some thoughtful minds. It is said, "When he is old he will not depart from the way he should go;" and they have found a difficulty as to the verification of this statement. They have cited instances of the best of men who have been afflicted with undutiful children; here a father, who has presented to the view of his sons a spotless example, and there a mother, who has given to her daughters the most excellent instructions, have mourned over early hopes blighted by the bad conduct of their offspring. "How then," they ask, "*can* the words of the text be true?" How can they be made to tally with the facts of common life? Still, they are true, for they state a general law which has as few exceptions as any law of the moral world. In that class of cases just now alluded to, however, the precept was not complied with; for there was not in reality such an education of the whole nature as deserves to be designated by the graphic phrase, "a training up in the way he should go." Lecturing, commanding, entreating, teaching, or setting a good example, is not *training*; but it is to use all these and other means of influence, so as to produce right HABITS OF ACTION, which is the essential thing in this important work. What is it to *train up* a child to be a musician? Is it merely to give him instructions on the theory of music? No. Is it merely to set before him an example of fine execution? No. Is it merely to combine these two things? No. In the days of youth we might all of us have heard the best lectures on music, and have witnessed daily examples of its execution by the most celebrated masters both in the school and concert-room, and yet might never have become musicians ourselves. Even if by dint of art and effort we had learned to perform a part for some particular occasion, we should soon have forgotten it, just because there had been no *training*, no formation of the habits. In accomplishing this task, the voice of the child is always exercised with artistic skill; he is drilled on his lessons; his taste is cultivated; his fingers are habituated to touch the instrument with effect, and he is taught to realize in action the ideas suggested to his mind, so that what at first was a slow and hard task is performed with ease and grace, as if it were the product of a second nature. How often at the outset has it seemed as if the child had no musical faculty whatsoever; and yet, in due time, after careful discipline, with what electrical speed has he been seen to sweep the chords of a capacious instrument, and to draw from it such sweetly expressive sounds that one might fancy the mechanism itself to be full of life and sympathy! This is all the achievement of a well-educated habit. Just so, with an enlarged application of the principle, to "train up a child in the way he should go," is not merely to furnish him with good rules or a good example, but to unite both; and then to form the *habits* of the child in harmony with them by seeing that ideas are realized in action. And if this be done, think you that when the child comes to be "old" he will scale every barrier, and rend every cord of just restraint which good habits have thrown around him, and by which they have upheld and guided him in the days of his youth and prime? As well might you expect "the Ethiopian to change his skin, or the leopard his spots." If such a case should occur, it would attract attention like a monstrosity in nature; like the African Albino, who, being a striking exception to the law of color, made on the mind of every beholder a fresh impression of the firmness and extent of that law's operation.

II. The proverb, then, fitly expresses the results of a wide observation and of a sound philosophy on the dominion of habit and on the importance of using this element of power in the formation of the charac ter. But in doing this, to what subordinate aims should our efforts be directed?

1. Essential to success, from every point of view, is the establishment of the *habit of obedience* on the part of the child at an early period. If it be not secured at an early period, the probability is, that it will not be acquired at all. And if it never be acquired, there is but little hope of effectually addressing the reason; for self-will and passion shall have so far gotten the start of you, that they will not allow the voice of parental remonstrance a calm and impartial hearing. You cannot address the reason of a child until the period arrive which nature has set for its healthy development by gradual exercise; but before that time shall have come, the child may be made the sport of capricious impulses, or the victim of rampant passions. These must be checked and regulated by parental *authority* alone; else they will soon gain the mastery, and amidst their harsh din the voice of reason will be unheard, and its power will be crushed by their rude tyranny. Perhaps this end may be attained without severity; but if not, then severity in a tender parent is the highest form of love. It was the counsel of true wisdom, we may be assured, that was uttered in the ancient saying, "Chasten thy son *while there is hope*, and let not thy soul spare for his crying."

One of the greatest difficulties in the way of carrying out this advice occurs when a child is weak and sickly, and perhaps afflicted with an irritable nervous temperament. In that case its very sallies of impetuous passion make their appeals to pity. But even then, when parental authority puts forth its demand of obedience with a calm and firm administration, it acts in mercy to the child. Such an authority, well-established, is the only proper counterprise to the force of those stormy agitations which sometimes rack the feeble frame of the little one, so as not merely to increase its misery, but to endanger its life. Have you never seen this illustrated in the nursery or the sick-chamber? I could tell you of an instance in which an unfortunate boy, at once the victim of disease and of an exasperated temper, refused to take the medicine which the physician had prescribed. The mother, who was wont to indulge him in every thing, had lost all control over him. All remonstrances, entreaties, and promises of reward were alike in vain. It was a sad spectacle. Matters were fast coming to a serious pass; for there the little fellow lay upon his bed in a state of fearful irritability, while the disease was every hour extending its ravages. It was then that the father, just returned from a journey, after a few days' absence from home, entered the room. He soon saw the real state of things. It had always been his rule to lay upon his children as few commands as possible, but at the same time never to allow a positive command to be disregarded. This was well understood even by the youngest. In his intercourse with them he was usually affable and playful; but when that particular tone fell upon the ear in the calm utterance of a command, it was always followed by prompt obedience. This salutary *habit* now developed its power. In its very formation the true ends of severity had already been gained, and severity was now no longer necessary. The established habit saved the boy. The father approached the bed with a look that expressed his meaning, and the announcement of his command carried the point at once. The impetuous passion that was feeding the fever-fires as they coursed through the veins was quelled immediately; the remedy was administered, refreshing sleep followed in due time, and the child's life was preserved. Surely, the establishment of such a supreme parental authority, so benign in its effect, was worth all the efforts and the pains it may have cost.

But suppose for a moment that this parent had been one of that class of persons who adopt the modern notion that no command must be enforced, and that a child must be left to have his own way, until the reason can be addressed. It is likely that the life of the suffering boy would have been made a sacrifice to the theory. This error of opinion is often openly advocated in our day, but it leads to practical mistakes which sometimes prove fatal, not only to the order of a family, but to the mental health and peace of children, and to the formation of all manly or womanly character. When ungoverned passions riot in the breast, they turn all the sweetnesses of life into poisonous gall; and yet,

> When reason, like the skilful charioteer,
> Can break the fiery passions to the bit,
> And, spite of their licentious sallies, keep
> The radiant track of glory, passions then
> Are aids and ornaments.

But let it be remembered that the passions are strong

before the reason is matured, and that parental authority is the chief power which God has appointed for their regulation and control.

2. In this connection I proceed to observe that the next point to be regarded in the management of a child is the cultivation of that *habit of self-direction*, without which all modes of education must fail of attaining their proper end. It should ever be kept in view that the chief aim of all parental rule is to qualify the child for self-government. Some kind of government is always necessary; for even the *man* who has no power of self-direction must be guided by others; and in relation to the child, the parents' hands may relax the reins just in proportion as they see him growing up to the proper management of himself. In observing the development of youthful character, this great test of the value of all educational training should be steadily regarded. A boy may appear very well while he is constrained to subject himself to domestic rules, and is accustomed to depend upon his parents for advice in all things; but unless he gradually acquire the power of *self-direction*, there is a mere show of education without the reality. Will he not be exposed, ere long, to enticing temptations? Will he not be obliged to cope with the arts of designing persons? Will he not be called to decide grave questions for himself? How to train up a child so as to bear responsibility, to act promptly and fitly in emergencies, is one of the most weighty problems which the parental relation suggests.

From this point of view, it is clear that there may

be too much government as well as too little. In order to train up a child to exercise this power of self-direction, he must be placed at times in situations which, in minor matters, will require him to act upon his own responsibility, and will put to the test, somewhat, his inclination, his tastes, his judgment and discretion. One of the finest exemplifications of this rule which we have ever known, was in the case of a mother who was accustomed to consult her young daughter on every occasion wherein it was possible to do so, just as if the girl had been capable of aiding her deliberations; and that, too, merely for the purpose of developing the child's judgment in a practical manner. Thus also, have I known a father who would arrange errands and commissions for his son in such a way as to try the aptitude of the boy to meet emergencies; and then, by censuring or approving the steps he had taken, sought to educate his self-directing power. The process was commenced in early years, and was not without effect in the formation of reliable character. Sometimes a kindly criticism of his son's mistakes and failures in a case where success had been made to appear very desirable, would accomplish more than a thousand general lectures. For it is worthy of observation that oftentimes a person, either old or young, may *seem* to have ample knowledge on matters that relate to conduct in life, and yet may fail at the point of action to put that knowledge forth in practice, on account of some cherished fault, weakness, or inadvertence, against which an apt parental discipline would have formed a lasting safeguard.

3. Another object to be pursued by means of domestic training, is the cultivation of a *love of truth*. In order to attain this effectually, the moral culture must be begun at an early period. For there is not a single vice which the human conscience more universally condemns than lying; and there is not one more universally indulged. In some children this bad propensity very early displays itself, because the temptations to its indulgence occur under the parental roof as well as elsewhere. Yet, in regard to this criminal habit there is a great difference of constitutional tendencies, even between those who are twin-born and who are daily companions throughout the whole course of childhood. In the same family one may be seen exhibiting a faculty of carrying his points by cunning and trickery, so as to be habitually tempted to speak with lying lips, and another under the same treatment will be free from all arts of evasion, inclined to speak at all times with that frank and open heart which wins universal confidence. But in spite of all natural diversities, there is no security for the maintenance of a truthful spirit amidst the snares and the excitements of life, except in that culture of the conscience which leads it to recognize the supremacy of the law of God. However finely constituted and balanced the natural faculties and affections may appear to be, there will be seen, at last, a fatal failure, if this principle be disregarded. In the family of the patriarch Isaac, we see an Esau possessing naturally a bold, manly, transparent character, and a Jacob insidious and deceptive from his early youth. In the one case we behold a man en-

dowed with the noblest gifts of nature rejecting the dominion of religious principle, without disguise and without shame selling his birthright for a mess of pottage; in the other, a man of greater constitutional faults subjecting himself to the redeeming power of true religion, and rising, comparatively, to the stature of manly dignity and moral perfection. From this ancient fragment of domestic history we are clearly taught that a human mind, cast in the very finest mould of Nature, without the renovating power of religious principle, will become the slave and victim of "the evil that dwelleth in it;" and, also, that another, constituted with the very worst dispositions and tendencies, may, by divine grace, gain the mastery of them, may feel the joy of "saving health," and put forth that force of moral character which will render one's memory a precious heritage for ever.

Probably, in nothing that relates to the formation of a moral habit, does so much depend on commencing at an early period. After a few years' indulgence of the practice of deception, the conscience becomes callous, and the mind loses the power of perceiving the nature and the evil of the thing. Some of the most accomplished villains that the world has seen, who, after a long career of prosperous wickedness, have been confronted by the effects of their cherished sin in the legal penalties of fraud, forgery, or perjury, have been brought to solemn reflection; and then, they have been able to trace their whole course of degradation to the first lie that was uttered in childhood beneath the parental roof. That first lie! It may have been uttered with faltering lips or with the smile of sportive mischief; it may have taken the form of deliberate trickery to gain a selfish end, or the form of a jest, dazzling by its brilliant wit; if discovered, it may have been treated as a matter of small account, unworthy of rebuke; but then, it has proved itself to have been a noxious seed from which has sprung up a bitter harvest of shame and woe. Let those, therefore, who have the management of a child, cultivate in its heart *the love of truth;* let them see that it becomes a ruling power of the mind, expressing itself in actions and manners as well as in speech, developing itself in plays and pastimes as well as on grave occasions; deeming no incidents that are adapted to strengthen it or put it to the test as too trivial to be noticed, but remembering that "he who despiseth little things shall fall by little and little."

4. Another object to be regarded in home-education is the training of the child to *habits of industry.* These are essential equally to happiness and to usefulness. To the child of fortune and the child of poverty they are alike necessary. The greater proportion of idlers who hang as "dead weight" upon society proceed from the ranks of those who occupy the two extremes of abounding wealth and abject poverty. But in either case, idleness is a source of misery. There is no deadlier bane of character. What spectacle can be more melancholy than that of a mind that is habitually unemployed, without an object to interest its attention or call its affections into healthful play? Its energies become introverted; it preys upon itself; it is the victim of *ennui;* it enjoys more happiness in sickness than

in health, if it can be properly said to have health at all; for it is a terrible truth commemorated by the poet who has said,

> **The vacant bosom's wilderness**
> **Will thank the pang that makes it less.**

Hence, if parents would save their children from a state of helpless misery that is likely to come upon them in spite of all outward advantages, let them begin betimes to cultivate habits of industrious occupation. This is a matter of practical importance which commends itself more urgently to those heads of families who reside in cities than it does to those whose home is in the country. For, in the circumstances of the former class there are greater difficulties to be overcome, because in days of childhood a city life furnishes but narrow scope for the exercise of a healthy activity. In the country it is otherwise; a farm is a capital school for the education of all the faculties in a useful direction, and it is very easy to cultivate in children a taste for rural pursuits. It is congenial with their nature, and is of inestimable value on account of its general influence on character. The majority of prosperous men in every city were born and brought up in the country. Inherited wealth changes hands more often here than there. This fact enfolds many a lesson; and among the reasons which may be assigned for its existence, the habits of industry which are formed by country life must hold a prominent place. Let parents remember, therefore, that a taste for industry is a most healthful virtue; that idleness is a sin and shame; and that the old Scripture-saying is as true now as ever: "The desire of the idle KILLETH him, because his hands refuse to labor."

5. Moreover, it should be the aim of the parent to cherish in the heart of the child a love of home that shall "grow with his growth," and become by habit the ruling passion of his "second nature." When the parental household realizes, in regard to the child, the true idea of a *home*, the very sound of the word becomes music to his ear; it stirs the heart of youth like an enchanting melody, softens the cares of manhood, and kindles rapture in the bosom of age. The strongest, the most self-relying and heroic men and women that have ever lived have been distinguished by this powerful sentiment. You may meet with wealthy loungers in foreign lands who seem to have no home; they are eager in the chase for pleasure; they rove from city to city; they drift with the impulses of fashion or fancy; but these genteel vagrants feel dreadfully the burden of life; they have no worthy object of pursuit, no moral centre around which their affections play, and they waste their energies on vain experiments to be happy. They verify the sober strain of a mirthful American poet:

He that is weary of his village plain
May rove the Edens of the world in vain;
'Tis not the star-crown'd cliff, or cataract's flow,
The softer foliage or the greener glow,
The lake of sapphire or the spar-hung cave,
The brighter sunset or the broader wave
Can warm his heart whom every breeze has blown
To every shore, forgetful of his own.

A child in whose heart the love of home has no place, lacks one of the strongest conservative principles of human character; and if God's special grace does not interpose to save him, he will surely become, like the doomed Cain, a vagabond in the earth.

The time that is included between twelve and twenty years of age is, in some respects, the most critical period of any one's moral history; for, although in the previous years a controlling bias may have been given to the character, the mind has not become so hardened in fixed habitudes but that fresh and lasting impressions may yet be made. And therefore, amidst all the new acquaintanceships and relationships that are then forming, spare no effort, no reasonable expense that may be requisite to keep your child's affections clustering around the home of his youth. Let it be made, as far as possible, a scene of employment and enjoyment. There let his healthy tastes find fit objects of gratification. There let his social nature joyously unfold itself. There let sympathetic and confiding intercourse throw its subtle spells around him. Let him have the management of his own property, however small its amount; whether it be merely a chest of tools, a museum, or a library. Let books, or music, or other proper means of recreation not be denied, if you have power to grant them. Alas, how many parents, in these things, are "penny-wise and pound-foolish!" How can we neutralize the power of those fatal enticements that beset the paths of the young on every side, except by investing the family-circle with the finest attractions that we may command?

For what if, through the harsh restraints and gloomy repulsiveness of the household, our sons and daughters seek their company and their recreations chiefly in other places? Who can tell what moral atmosphere they will inhale? Whether their associations shall be good or bad will be to us a mere matter of chance; and then, how easily all their lively sensibilities may become elements of ruin by being alienated from parents, brothers, sisters, friends, from the ways of virtue, from the sanctuary, and from God, by means of vile companionship! The more we consider this one aim of which we speak—by far too much overlooked—the more does it loom up to view with an aspect of impressive magnitude, so that in the pursuit of it there is no liability to extravagance; and therefore do we say, let this point be carried at any cost, since a failure here will be pretty sure to balk your efforts in every other direction.

6. Still further, it should be the constant aim of parents in domestic training to form the character of a child on the *basis of religious principle.* "Other foundation can no man lay." "The fear of the Lord is the beginning of wisdom." Here only is solid rock; "all is sea besides." Nothing else will beat back the surges of temptation, or endure the fiery trials of calamity and disappointment. The highest degree of worldly wisdom, the strongest incentives of worldly interest, the fondest associations of worldly friendship, will all give way in some emergencies; nothing can withstand the wear and tear of character in the sharp collisions and sirocco-like excitements of this changing life,

except the energy of religious faith. Even Infidelity itself, in its solemn moods, has paid its tribute of homage to religion, in the acknowledgment of this truth. Yes! as Voltaire has expressed it, "the LAW which follows a man beyond the sight of his fellows, and takes cognizance of the actions which are secret, is the law of religion;" and a sincere regard for this is essential to all effective self-government, whether of the community or the individual. There are times when nothing can hold the soul back from sin and crime except that principle in the heart which led the young Israelite to exclaim in the ear of the tempter, "How can I do this great wickedness, and sin against God?" On this account it is that the deliberate desecration of the Sabbath is so often the first step, in a descending series, of a long criminal career. With what a melancholy moan was this truth confessed by a New England pirate, in his dungeon, awaiting his execution, when he said, "Sabbath-schools came fifteen years too late for me." The time had been when he seemed incapable of the deeds which led him to the scaffold; and the most amiable youth who goes forth into the world without the guidance of religious principle has not sufficient power to cope with the wiles of sin, but will be likely, in an unexpected moment, to stumble, to fall, and "be destroyed without remedy."

Nevertheless, when the aims which have now been set forth are steadily pursued by means of religious culture, by the inculcation of the Saviour's teachings, by example, discipline, and prayer, the parents may *expect* success. O, let them remember that these must all be united. And in the employment of these means it becomes both the parents to act together. What a sad spectacle of domestic life is seen when one imparts religious instruction, and the other baffles it with ridicule or witticism; when one by means of example allures the young in the path to heaven, and the other treads the way of transgressors; when one aims to strengthen the child's character by a well-adjusted discipline, and the other weakens it by indulgence; when one seeks God's help by prayer, and the other turns away from the closet, the family-altar and the sanctuary! Hard are life's burdens then to the faithful parent, and life itself may be so to the poor child of their mutual love. Still, let the prayerful not faint, but continue to implore the grace of God. On the other hand, what a lovely scene is that which greets the eyes of angels and of men, when an intelligent and happy pair unite to train their offspring for the skies; when the healthful atmosphere of an earthly home prepares the young immortals who breathe it for the purer climate of the New Jerusalem; when the whole family are moving onward to the glorious destinations of that final day in which the faithful parents shall stand with joy before the throne of the universe, saying, "Lord, here are we and the children thou hast given us!"

Duties of Children to Parents.

"CHILDREN, OBEY YOUR PARENTS IN THE LORD: FOR THIS IS RIGHT. HONOR THY FATHER AND MOTHER, (WHICH IS THE FIRST COMMANDMENT WITH PROMISE,) THAT IT MAY BE WELL WITH THEE, AND THOU MAYEST LIVE LONG ON THE EARTH."—Ephesians vi. 1, 2, 3.

THE subject which I now approach is one which has an intimate connection with the welfare of every community, and claims for itself a share in the regards of every individual. We have all been called to the discharge of filial duties; for, although some of us may have been orphans from our infancy, there are, or there have been, those to whom we owe acknowledgments of gratitude for the care that they have taken of us. To this remark there are very few exceptions; and if it were so that many of us could cite our personal histories as furnishing cases of exception, even then, the motives of philanthropy and patriotism, not to say of religion, should lead us to cherish a sympathetic concern in seeing that filial duties are properly inculcated, understood, and practised. For, wheresoever these are neglected, wheresoever the prevailing tone of social sentiment treats them lightly, there, public immorality, rampant passions, crime and disorder will surely reign like fiends keeping an incessant carnival. As in the house of Eli, the insubordination of his sons arrayed the agencies of Providence against the family, so that they fell together in a common overthrow, thus, in a community, the prevalence of unrestrained self-will in childhood will dissolve the ties of society, and issue in a general ruin. "Honor thy father and thy mother," is the first commandment of the second table of the law, and the first to which is annexed a promise of prosperity. Although the rewards of filial obedience are not so obvious now, in relation to individuals, as they were under the Jewish economy, yet the temporal welfare of a nation or a community is seen to be, now, as much as ever, dependent on fidelity to this precept. This established connection was not hidden from the view of the heathen world. A filial spirit was the leading feature of that ideal standard of virtue which the Romans celebrated in poetry and in song; a spirit fostered in youthful breasts by the story of their great ancestor, who, on account of the love he displayed in bearing an aged father on his shoulders away from the wreck of burning Troy, was distinguished in many a lyric strain as "the pious Æneas." And while the intelligent heathen can honor the beauty and grandeur of such a trait of character, God, in his written word, threatens a bad end to those who set it at naught. "The eye that mocketh at his father and despiseth to obey his mother, the ravens of the valley shall pluck it out and the young eagles shall eat it."

a sentence which gives forth the intimation that with an undutiful child the irrational creation, the elements of nature, and the workings of Providence shall surely be at war. But amongst all the enchanting pictures of social happiness which this world exhibits, is there one that stirs the heart with a delight more exquisite than that which is awakened by beholding a group of children, intelligent, amiable, affectionate, united in honoring their parents, ministering to their comfort amidst the infirmities that increase with advancing years, smoothing their pathway to the tomb, thus enabling them in the season of tremulous old age to renew their youth, and to live over their life again by identifying their very being with the prosperity of their offspring?

My young friends, already has it been my aim to lay before your parents a few considerations touching your welfare, suggested by the precepts, hints, and maxims of the Scriptures; allow me now to call your attention to the duties which you owe to them.

1. The first obligation that I urge upon you in this connection relates to the heart. Love your parents; and cherish this sentiment habitually as a *principle of action*, in spite of every opposing influence. Guard sedulously against every thing which would tend to wean your affections from them. In addressing parents, I did not lay much stress on the obligation to cherish parental love; for a parent's love is instinctive and controlling. As soon as the infant's cry reaches a mother's ear, she is conscious of a self-devoting love which can "endure all things;" which makes light of toil and weariness, tedious vigils, care and pain, and

deems no sacrifice too costly to be yielded for the well-being of its object. The love of the father, too, takes deeper root with advancing years; and, as the responsibility of support and counsel is made to press more weightily upon him by the expansion of youthful character, parental affections gain daily vigor without much effort for their cultivation. Even the most reckless and ungrateful conduct, instead of destroying them, will often develop their native strength; a truth illustrated by that plaintive strain which broke from the heart of David on the death of Absalom. Such is their vital force, that special care is requisite to give them a right direction. But that very love, in its earlier dealings with you, was obliged very often to cross your feelings, to control your passions, and, before you could in words express your wishes, to deny you many hurtful things which you sought to gain by sobs and tears. It was parental *love*, however, as real and as tender, when in time of sickness it administered the bitter medicine which you struggled against, as when at other times it won your smile by joining in your sports or by giving you curious toys and picture-books. In some of its aspects, therefore, it seemed to be *severe*, and failed, perhaps, to draw forth from you any return of grateful love. Nay, at times it may have provoked a degree of sullen anger; it may have roiled the springs of feeling so that they poured forth streams of bitterness. Hence, on your part, such love as they deserve, in order to thrive healthfully, must needs be cultivated. With the early dawn of reason you began to have the capacity of doing this; and the work of self-culture is carried forward by reflecting frequently on the relation which they sustain to you; by remembering how deep and abiding is the place which you hold in the heart of each of them; how much your misery would affect them; how much a surly word from you, or any rudeness of manner, must disturb their peace; how much their happiness is in your keeping; how much they have done for you and still would do to promote your welfare. If your sensibilities have become seared, cherished memories like these will quicken them afresh, and will stir, as if by some magical or seraphic touch, those finer chords of feeling that still lie hidden in the depths of your nature.

And as you now look abroad over the wide word, is it at all probable that, among its thousand millions of inhabitants, you can find one friend more disinterested in regard to your real welfare than your father or your mother? You may find many who are possessed of more talents, or more money, or more of certain qualities congenial with your tastes; you may find those who have it in their power to confer on you more signal benefits; but where can you find hearts that throb with so pure a love for you as those of your own parents? Oh, how often has it been seen in the course of human life that the youth whose affections had become estranged from his own family, who had gone like a "prodigal son" away from his father's house, who amidst scenes of success and gayety had found friends to flatter him and to bask in the sunshine which he could spread around them, after having become a broken-down and disappointed man, wrecked in health and fortune, after having become deserted and forlorn, has then returned with blasted hopes to receive the kindly sympathies which were as yet flowing but from a single source—a parent's heart!

If we take a look at the histories of men whom the world, at any period whatsoever, has owned to be truly great, it will appear to be worthy of notice how much all the rugged and sterner qualities of their character have been relieved, and harmonized into a pleasing unity, by the softening hue and glow which the grace of filial love has thrown around them. Humanity, everywhere, both in Pagan and Christian lands, acknowledges the moral power of this sentiment. The study of Grecian history afforded to the educated classes of the Roman people a pleasure as intense as that which is enjoyed by the scholars of our own land; and, among the leading men of Greece, to whom did the Romans award the palm of excellence! Cicero affirms that Epaminondas was the greatest of them all. But then, let it be remembered that filial virtue was the crowning glory of this noble Theban; for, when he was asked on the day of his most signal triumph what it was that gratified him most, he replied, that it was the consideration of that pure joy with which his success would be hailed by his father and his mother. By that confession he has won his way to the hearts of mankind, who have always delighted to honor him because he never sunk the character of the man in that of the soldier or the statesman. A similar tribute of admiration has been, and ever will be, paid to our own Washington, whose profound regard for his mother, cherished amid all the cares of the camp, and all the splendors of civil dignity, indicated that simplicity of real manliness which is an essential element of true greatness.

The master painters of Europe have found favorite themes for the pencil in those incidents which distinguish the simple story of the patriarch Joseph, and which lay hold of every reader as by the fascination of romance; but there is no scene of that touching biography more worthy to be pictured on the canvas by the hand of Genius than that wherein the viceroy of Egypt exhibits the spirit of filial heroism, while he l[illegible] the good old shepherd and wayworn pilgrim into the court of Pharaoh, and with grateful pride presents him to the monarch as his father. One of the finest relics of ancient pastoral poetry is that lyrical strain of Ruth in which she breathes forth her spirit of devotion to Naomi, her bereaved mother-in-law. "Entreat me not to leave thee, or to return from following after thee; for whither thou goest I will go, and where thou lodgest I will lodge: thy people shall be my people, and thy God my God: where thou diest will I die, and there will I be buried; the Lord do so to me, and more also, if aught but death part thee and me." This filial sentiment, whether it appear in man or woman, invests one's character with an aspect of beauty, dignity, and sacredness. How much it must have elevated royalty itself in the eyes of all, when it was announced to Solomon, while at the height of his power, that his mother asked an audience of him: "And the king rose up to meet her, and bowed himself unto her, and sat down on his throne, and caused a seat to be set for the king's mother; and she sat on his right hand." Such an act of filial reverence as this is adapted to win the sympathies of man universally, whether he be in a state of civilization or of barbarism; for every human being whose heart has not been paralyzed by vice or crime will unite in the wish so well expressed in Pope's celebrated strain:

"Me let the tender office long engage
To rock the cradle of reposing age;
With lenient arts extend a mother's breath,
Make languor smile, and smoothe the bed of death;
Explore the thought, explain the asking eye,
And keep awhile one parent from the sky."

2. Having taken a proper care that the ground-work of a truly filial character be laid in the principle of love, resolve, I pray you, practically and habitually to regard the command which enjoins *obedience* to your parents. In doing this, set before your view a high standard of attainment. Be not content with moping inefficiency. Aim at perfection, in spite of all failures to reach it; like the artist, who, when he detects the blemishes of his work, renews his efforts for improvement. The divine precept is, "Children, obey your parents in the Lord; for this is right." Every mind is so constituted as to see at once that it is in harmony with the laws of nature that the young and inexperienced should obey the older and the wiser; and besides, independently of these qualities of condition, that the parental relation itself lays an additional obli-

gation on the conscience. In helpless childhood obedience is a necessity. The young of all animals, whether they be beasts or birds, wild or domesticated, are instinctively obedient. The eagle "stirring up her nest," in order to teach her young to fly; the hen gathering her obedient brood beneath her wings, in order to shield them from danger, have furnished to the ancient poets some of their choicest imagery. But in the education of the human race, as children with advancing years become capable of resistance, obedience is enjoined as a DUTY, and is expected as a free tribute of the heart and conscience, because "it is right."

This obedience, let us observe, young friends, in order to have any real worth, so as to be pleasing to God or man, must be *voluntary* and cheerful. A precept may be fulfilled to the very letter with minute exactness, and yet the beauty of obedience may be destroyed by sullenness. This is folly; it is a wanton waste of the means of happiness, very much like that which appeared in the case of an eminent man, of whom it was observed just after he had conferred on another an important favor, "He always spoils a good thing by the rough and hateful manner of his doing it!" So a sullen or a murmuring compliance with a parent's wish, carries on its face no aspect of pleasantness. That which is worth doing at all is worth doing well. Spoil nothing by ill-grace. "Let not your good be evil spoken of." To obey when the direction chimes exactly with your own inclination is a thing that may very easily be done; but to deny yourself, to school your feelings into a ready subjection to parental authority, is a task which furnishes a fine opportunity for the discipline of the heart, and for the formation of a self-governing character. And in the relation which you occupy, this is the very work your Maker requires of you. The youth who does this, strengthens within his heart the principle of rectitude. He learns to act habitually in view of what is RIGHT. He is forming gradually a noble, manly, and enduring character, which will render him the strength and joy of his parents in their declining years, will qualify him to resist temptation, to bear misfortune, to improve success, to enjoy aright the sunshine of life, or brave its desolating storms.

In accordance with the teachings of Scripture, obedience should be *universal.* "Children, obey your parents in the Lord *in all things.*" The terms here used deserve attention from this point of view, because they imply that to this law of filial obedience there may be just cases of exception. The exception which the terms imply is that of a case wherein a command is contrary to the known will of God. In such a case, compliance would not be obeying our parents *in the Lord.* Then, obedience would be wrong. A parent should be careful never to constrain a child to act against his conscience. Admitting that the child's conscience be erroneous, it is not to be corrected by force. The error may be unfortunate, but in the long run, force will only make the matter worse by confirming that error, and by awakening in the youthful breast the resistance of a martyr-spirit. If any of you, my young friends, should ever be constrained, unhappily, to differ from your parents in regard to principles of religion, or the performance of a religious duty, let me commend to you two important rules of action. (1.) The first is, that you should resolve to submit to them as far as you possibly can do so, while under age, without offending God. Renounce, if it be necessary, every thing that may be regarded as a mere privilege; if you pursue a course that is opposed to their wishes, let it be only in obedience to the voice of Duty. We have a fine example of this rule in the story of the lad who was bidden by his father to commit an act of theft, by taking some small article that was the property of another. The son expressed some fear that he might be detected. "Put it in your pocket," said the father. "God can see in my pocket," answered the conscientious boy, and thus maintained his integrity. (2.) Then, again, in all cases where parental authority seems to come in conflict with that which is Divine, let your conduct be meek, quiet, courteous, and obliging. Guard well your temper, words, manners, and the general spirit of your deportment. If your parents perceive that your actions proceed from right feelings of heart, from the supreme dictates of conscience, and profound reverence for God, they will probably sustain you by their kindly sympathies, although they may not coincide with your religious opinions. Have a special care, in such a case as this, that you exhibit the spirit of true religion *at home*, in all the manifold forms of filial and domestic virtue, so that you shall thus illustrate Christianity in daily life, and "adorn the doctrine of God in all things." Then, if, on the one hand, you shall have been misled by some false views as to the course of duty, you will be most likely to discover and correct your errors; and, on the other hand, if your "steps shall have taken hold of the way of truth," you will find your way irradiated by increasing light, and your heart cheered by more signal tokens of the favor of Heaven. If God be for you, who can be against you?

3. In addition to these leading and subordinate precepts, Christianity requires that you HONOR your parents by spontaneous and generous efforts to promote their happiness. Others may honor them as friends, as neighbors, citizens, or members of society; but whether others do so or not, it is yours to honor them as *parents* by a studious accommodation of your conduct to their tastes and wishes. Even though you may think them to be deficient in many things, such as mental strength, knowledge, or judgment, yet the parental relation requires you to pay respect to their opinions and their feelings. It is a revolting spectacle that some households have exhibited, when parents whose lot in early life has been a lot of toil and hardship, having used the means which they have industriously acquired in order to impart to their children the best education which the country could furnish, have then been thoughtlessly ridiculed by those very children on whom they had lavished their money in conferring superior advantages. Such young persons painfully verify the old Grecian fable which tells us of a countryman who kindly placed a frozen serpent in his

bosom, warmed it into life, and then suffered from its sting. Too often, indeed, such a sad result might have been anticipated from the influence of some fashionable boarding-schools, which cultivate the intellect, the imagination, and a taste for showy accomplishments, but which actually benumb the moral sense, and leave the heart like an aboriginal wilderness, luxuriant only in the beauteous bloom of poisonous vines and flowering briers. But then, to the eyes of every true-hearted man or woman, there is no sight more grateful and refreshing than that of children who, having enjoyed fine opportunities of education, do all that lieth within their power to conceal the defects and blemishes of a parent, and challenge for the parental character the fit tributes of honor and esteem.

Let it not be forgotten that the rule which requires you to honor your parents implies a due regard to your *manners* in their presence. For often, when one's words are decorous, the expression of the countenance, the tones of the voice, the general bearing and deportment leave a disagreeable impression. It is a great mistake which some commit to treat these things as unworthy of notice, for they are really essential elements of that home-life whose subtle influence hangs around our spirits as a murky and depressing gloom, or quickens them like a genial and invigorating atmosphere.

In following out this precept, it may be requisite that you should aid your parents by your habitual *industry*. If so, do it with a willing heart and a ready hand. Who can tell how much it may be in your power to make the course of household affairs run smoothly? We have often seen that the placid temper and the cheerful services of a child are like oil on the springs and wheels of some delicate machinery, allaying much of its harsh friction, and saving much of the "wear and tear" to which it is liable. Whensoever any errands are committed to you, however minute they may be, perform them promptly. Cherish a habit of *punctuality*. Avoid being drones in any thing; but whatsoever you undertake, aim to do it well. If you are made the bearer of a message, deliver it correctly; if an answer is to be returned, be careful not to forget it or mistake its meaning. If any service like this be expected of you, why should you loiter by the way, to waste your time in talk, or play, or in gazing at the shop-windows? In all these matters, you are forming, during the season of youth, those habits which shall rule over you in following years, and establish your character, for good or for evil, throughout the whole course of life.

Honor their *opinions*, too, as to those matters which concern your welfare. Do not tease them for money, or for expensive dress, or for indulgences which they cannot grant with a good conscience and a willing heart. It is not without reason that I speak of these things; for, even now, I can well remember one of my school-mates who would often boast that he could always "carry his points" with his father, so as to get any thing that he desired. In the school it was a common saying that he was "flush in cash;" his pockets and his desk were generally filled with costly confectionery which he would distribute liberally. Thus he gained many friends; for he was naturally generous. His youth seemed to pass like one bright holiday; and, on this account, how often have I known him to be envied by the other scholars, whose parents were less wealthy, or less indulgent! But, after all, the retrospect is a gloomy one. This whole course of gratification was ruinous to my young companion, who, in early manhood, became the victim of morbid appetites; "a hale fellow well-met" in the circles of fashionable dissipation, and then "died before his time." He was destroyed by indulgence. The whole story of his untimely end may be compressed into this single statement: the kind-hearted boy was too successful in persuading his parents to yield to all his wishes, contrary to the dictates of their better judgment.

Moreover, my young friends, since I have not forgotten to suggest to your parents that it is their duty to consult for your happiness by furnishing you, *at home*, with all the means of enjoyment which they may properly command, I may now freely say to you that the honor which you owe to them requires that you should consult their feelings in regard to the *company* that you invite to the house. Be careful not to grieve them by introducing into the family-circle associates whose character your parents cannot approve, and whose influence they may dread. A similar remark applies to the *books* which you may carry home; for, if their love for you is breathed in prayers for your welfare, would they not be troubled to see you disposed to give up your mind and time to the reading of such vile trash as passes under the name of "new novels," of popular literature composed by unprincipled men whose trade it is to pander to the lowest passions—men who would not hesitate, if they had the chance, to take your life by poison or the dagger, in order to obtain the means of one night's revel?

Having thus called your attention, as far as the limits of this occasion will allow, to the duties of the filial relation, let me add, that if any of them should hereafter seem to be irksome, or to require the exercise of self-denial, fail not, at such a time, to remember how much a regard to *your* happiness has been to your parents an incentive to toil and self-sacrifice. Many a father who has been as one wearied unto death by the cares of business, weak and faint in spirit while grappling with difficulties, on the point of sinking into gloomy despondency, has been nerved to hard endurance by the sight or thought of his children, by the desire to prepare them for a happy and a useful life. Your mother, too, loves you as no earthly being can love. Had she spared herself, cared for her own ease, and remitted her watchful oversight of you during many a tedious night of your infancy, you might have been now halting as a cripple, or groping as the blind, or pining with disease, or moving about with the vacant stare of idiocy. Surely, then, a filial spirit is one element of real manliness; a truth which the world has acknowledged in its admiration of that sentiment which was expressed by Alexander the Great to his friend Antipater, in answer to letters filled with complaints touching the conduct of Olympias, the monarch's mother.

"Knowest thou not that one tear of my mother will blot out a thousand such letters."

But then, while you lay to heart these filial obligations, and resolve that you will aim with all diligence to fulfil them, remember, I pray you, your dependence on the grace of God for the strength that you need in order to carry into effect your own determinations. For all our determinations to do good, or to pursue a virtuous course, may seem to have a mighty force while we enjoy the musings of our quiet retreats, or while we are surrounded with social influences that are congenial with our better feelings. Nevertheless, the time of trial, "the hour and power of darkness," will come to all. The pleasures, the cares, the excitements of life, the development of latent tastes and passions, absence, distance, new scenes, and new society, will furnish many a temptation to neglect or violate our best resolutions. Religious principle, or, as the Scriptures express it, "the grace of God which bringeth salvation," is the only reliable source of moral energy. This endures for ever. To impart this to man, Jesus Christ came into the world. Every change in human life, every example of human weakness, every new phase of human experience, discloses a deeper significance in that monitory lesson which He has given unto us: "Abide in me, and I in you; as the branch cannot bear fruit except it abide in the vine, no more can ye, except ye abide in me." No man cometh unto the Father but by Him. Will you not, therefore, with a simple-hearted, childlike faith, commit yourself to his guidance? Since it requires no very careful observation to behold around us on every side the withered buds of early promise, the blight of parental hopes, the deadly blast and utter ruin of many a youthful character, "Wilt thou not from this time cry unto Him, My Father, thou art the guide of my youth?"

Duties of Brothers and Sisters.

"BEHOLD HOW GOOD AND HOW PLEASANT IT IS FOR BRETHREN TO DWELL TOGETHER IN UNITY."—Psalm cxxxiii. 1.

THE very word *brother* has a sound which stirs the heart. Where is there a human bosom that is utterly insensible to the power of its appeal? The Arab of the Eastern deserts, and the Indian of the Western forests, alike answers to its call; and if a stranger in a strange land, whether amidst the marts of commerce or the solitudes of the Rocky Mountains, should hear a human being of any tribe or color hailing him by that name, he would interpret it at once as the sign and pledge of friendship. Three thousand years ago, when a cause of contention arose between two chieftains on the fields of Canaan, the difficulty was removed by Abraham's saying unto Lot, "Let there be no strife between us, for we are brethren;" and ages afterwards, when Moses sought as a legislator to chasten the feelings of the Israelites towards a rival nation, he proclaimed, "Ye shall not abhor an Edomite, for he is thy *brother*." Even the man who has been brought up in his father's house as an only son, who in days of childhood had none to share with him the affections of his parents, when he has chanced to look abroad over the family groups of his acquaintance, and has observed the family likeness in their features while they were encircling their parents as a common centre of interest, has apprehended at a glance the endearments of such a relationship, and has felt how strong must be the ties which unite the hearts of those who, while under the parental roof, with all the simplicity of childhood, with all the frankness of confiding youth, and all the strengthening affections of riper years, have heard from each others' lips in daily intercourse the appellations of brother and sister. Naturally, in thought he transfers the name to those whom he loves as equals, and calls them brethren. And so universally is a kindred feeling roused in the human soul by this association of ideas, that when inspired poetry, predicting the final triumphs of truth, rises to its climax of description, it is satisfied to portray the warring clanships of earth as having disappeared in the embrace of one generous and world-wide brotherhood.

Once the world *was* one brotherhood. The first pages of sacred history exhibit the whole race as occupying the old Asiatic homestead, inherited from our first parents. There was then no slavery, no grinding poverty, no great diversity of form or complexion, arising from difference of habits, food, clothing, or climate. There was an equality of rank and condition. But the charm of this moral landscape was spoiled by sin, and with sin came misery, showing that neither inequality of rank, nor an unequal distribution of property, was the chief source of woe to man, according to the dream of some philosophical socialists. But in that family the oldest son cherished towards a younger one feelings of envy, hate, and wrath, and the first brother became the first murderer. What dread and horror must have thrilled the breasts of his parents when they saw his hands stained with fraternal blood, and thought of the deeper crimson of his soul! Discord, strife, and death there proclaimed the reign of sin, and to us they suggest the impressive lesson that, although the bonds of brotherhood formed by nature are very pleasant and very sacred, yet they may be rent apart by some ruthless passion, in an hour of excitement, like cords of "flax at touch of fire;" so that, in order to reap the love, peace, and joy which are the proper fruits of this relationship, we must rely on the influence of pure religion, on the cultivation of the conscience, the reason, and the affections, quickened, enlightened and directed by genuine Christianity.

Remembering, then, that however richly endowed we may be by nature with amiable sentiments, we must needs consider the duties that arise from the relation of brothers and sisters in order to exemplify them, let us inquire what these are, with the purpose of strengthening our sense of obligation to observe them.

1. Cultivate practically, and by all right means, that magnanimous love which is congenial with the relation of brother or sister. "Doth not nature itself teach" us that this relation was designed by the Creator to be a spring of tender affections? If it be natural for the heart of a youth to turn with fondness towards the

parent on whom he depends for sustenance and care, is it natural to turn away with coldness from those who share that parent's love? If a filial spirit rule as it ought to do in the bosom of a child, can there be in that same bosom an utter lack of fraternal feeling where the relation of brotherhood exists to call it forth? True love, regarded as to its essential nature, implies a sympathy with its object, and a desire to please; and as the Scripture saith that he who loves God must love his Christian brother also, undoubtedly he who loves an earthly parent will love those who share that parent's heart. And if the destitution of a filial spirit implies the lack of any solid ground on which to rear a noble and manly character, the brother who has no fraternal love is unfitted for all the social connections and duties of life. This remark is applicable, of course, to the character and condition of the sister who is destitute of the affections which this relation is adapted to inspire. Supremely selfish in her sentiments and aims, and the whole "spirit of her mind," she will be likely to realize in action the idea expressed in the lines of an old English poet:

> "She hath neither manners, honesty, behavior,
> Wifehood, nor womanhood."

That a magnanimous and enduring love is congenial with the nature of this relation, is clearly evident from the fact that it involves so many interests that are common to those who hold it to each other. They are concerned alike in the *good name* of their parents, which to them "is better than great riches;" in the *reputation of the family*, wherein if one suffer, all the members suffer with that one; in the success of the *father*, while he struggles amid the din of business to gain a livelihood, or by prudence to manage his property; in the health and happiness of the *mother*, whose watchful eye and presiding mind are necessary to direct the affairs of the household. All these furnish common grounds to the fraternal circle for hope or fear, joy or sorrow—for mutual incitement or restraint—and justify on the part of each a friendly remonstrance with the other for any course of conduct which may jar against the harmony of the whole, or be adverse to the common welfare.

All this will appear more evidently still to any one who will array within his view the common objects of family life that are fitted to awaken in the mind of each touching reminiscences of the past, anticipations of the future, and those kindred feelings which constitute bonds of sympathy. Fraternal recollections go back to the *nursery*, where in the season of infancy each was watched by the same eyes, in hours of suffering partook of the same guardian care, was lulled to sleep by the same song, reposed in the same arms or on the same pillow; to the *school*, where each was called to grapple with the same tasks, aud to cope with similar difficulties; to the *playground*, so dear to memory as the bright and pleasant spot where all joined together, or with their fellows, in the same childish sports; to the *table* where each had his place, and his plate or cup, received food dispensed by the same hands, and basked in the sunshine of the same countenances which illumined the common centre of family meeting and enjoyment; to the familiar *friends* who were welcomed to the father's house, and beguiled there many an evening hour, or gave their aid in time of trouble; to scenes of sickness, where all turned with anxious gaze to the same *couch*, approached it with a like gentle step, and watched the symptoms with kindred apprehensions; and, perhaps, though this to many of us may be yet to come, to the same parental *funeral*, where all looked for the last time on the face of that best earthly friend, whose heart had embraced them all as one; then turned away to move towards the same *grave* which was opened to receive the object of their common veneration, and where they still meet in spirit, while memory lingers there with mingled emotions of gratitude, love, and pensive sorrow. Whensoever we walk through a cemetery as new as that which adorns our own neighborhood, where spacious tombs have been prepared, and places arranged within them, to receive all the members of the family now mingling here in the scenes of active, joyous life, how affecting is the lesson uttered by the stony lips of the monuments above them, reminding us that the parents and children who now occupy the same house upon the surface of the earth shall soon meet in a dark and narrow one beneath it, to share a common destiny, to blend in kindred dust.

Now, who that considers all these incentives to domestic unity which God has furnished to us all in the constitution and course of nature, can fail of seeing that it was his desire that those who are united by such tender, sacred, and enduring ties, should cherish towards each other a peculiar affection, more intimate and confiding than that of ordinary friendship; and that for such as these to meet each other with averted looks or hearts of strife is a revolting spectacle, a heinous and a deadly sin?

2. Hence, I am led to observe that the law of brotherhood enjoins it as a duty that you quench that spirit of JEALOUSY which sometimes enters stealthily a peaceful home, and disturbs the youthful circle around their parents' hearth. Wheresoever it is indulged, it paralyzes every generous feeling; yea, poisons the life-blood of the social nature. In the daily routine of affairs in every family there are constantly arising those occasions which seem exactly adapted to afford genial aliment to this spirit of evil, if it be at all harbored in the bosom. The first sign of its existence in the heart of a child may well alarm our fears; for it grows with one's growth, and keeps the inventive faculties of considerate parents constantly on the rack in order to avoid the appearance of partiality. The victim of this feeling is ever imagining that others are better treated than himself; for it has been truly said,

> It is jealousy's peculiar nature
> To swell small things to great; nay, out of thought
> To conjure much, and then to lose its reason
> Amid the hideous phantoms it has formed.

Be alert, therefore, to quench the first spark of this subtle and wasting passion. First of all cherish a generous faith in your parents' love; it is due to them. Concede much to their discretion. "Honor thy father and thy mother" is the first command with promise; and let it be yours to honor them by confiding in their kind intentions towards *you*, as well as towards your brothers or sisters. If they adopt any distinguishing treatment, attribute it to any motive that is possible rather than that of petty favoritism. Do not tease them for explanations; for they cannot always announce the reasons for every little plan or project which they may wish to carry out in action.

Then, again, guard carefully against that leaven of egotism which sometimes leads one member of a family to speak more of himself and to claim more for himself than others may think to be proper. Here, it may appear in one's demanding particular attentions or privileges because he is the oldest; there, in another's doing it because he is the youngest, having been, on that account, perhaps too much petted and indulged. A third, or a fourth, may set up some other plea; and, ere long, this selfish spirit, if unrebuked, is sure to introduce into the family-circle its own natural offspring, disaffection, sullenness, and strife. Watch against it. Resist it. Unmask it, whatsoever guise it may wear. Drive it from every lurking-place, for it will make your heart like a nest of serpents. A filial spirit nourished by religious principle is the best medicine to destroy its venom. By the aid of divine grace, resolve that as far as you are concerned peace shall reign at home; that there shall be one place on earth where this selfish and corroding passion shall not have it way. For this, "deny thyself and take thy cross;" so shalt thou have a better treasure than can be gained by carrying a selfish policy against the dictates of conscience, the commands of Heaven, the hopes of parents, and the claims of fraternal love.

But why do I speak, in this connection, of a better mental treasure to be gained by this kind of self-denial? Is it merely, think you, in view of the present calm and inward sunshine imparted by an approving conscience? That, indeed, is much; but the benefit of that spirit which I commend to you stretches far onward to the destinies of future life. For jealousy, indulged at home, will destroy all the finer feelings of the soul, and will corrode the interior elements of the character as vitriol doth the flesh. Let it be your aim, therefore, to rise superior to it. Oppose it at the outset. Let it gain no advantage by subtlety or stealth. Because it hath been truly said that this, of all the passions,

> Exacts the hardest service, and pays
> The bitterest wages. Its service is,
> To watch an enemy's success ; its wages,
> To be sure of it.

The great importance of this lesson which I am now inculcating has been recognized by men of every class and every clime in its immediate bearing upon the earthly interests and honor of a family. In this one respect our own times have witnessed a remarkable instance of the value of fraternal unity. For the nations of Christian Europe have beheld the Rothschilds, an obscure Jewish family, rising up in their midst to put forth a power which has often been felt in deliberations touching the great questions of diplomacy. The financial business of that house began to assume importance in consequence of its first loan, of ten millions of florins, to the King of Denmark. In the year 1812, Mayer Anselmo Rothschild, the father, was attacked with a mortal illness. He called his children to his bedside, blessed them, then made them promise never to abandon their religion, and always to be *united on 'Change.* These promises have been kept; and it has been truly said, "Most amply has the fable of the bundle of sticks been verified by the five brothers." Their interests have been identical. They have swayed a golden sceptre; they have illustrated the power of capital when wielded with skill and in subordination to a steady aim. The principle of fraternal unity which they have exemplified on an immense scale of operation is applicable to the smallest sphere of action; and when it is guided by Christian wisdom and benevolence, who can tell what vast and benign results it may achieve? Had these money-kings been animated by a spirit of true religious philanthropy, and subordinated their splendid financial talents to the service of Christ, they might have adorned the face of the world wth the memorials of a useful beneficence more grand and glorious than any that have yet been seen within the whole range of human history. How many a barren waste might then have broken forth into joyous song like that which charms the ear in the strain of my text: How good and how pleasant it is for brethren to dwell together in unity!

3. In the development of this subject, let me ask you to observe still further, that it becomes children of the

same family to seek, day by day, to give free scope to their natural sympathies in acts of *courtesy* and mutual *assistance.* In the relationship of brothers and sisters young persons may reap those benefits which they can derive from no other source. The Creator has formed it as a means of healthful discipline for the wider sphere of this world's associations. The tributes of attention and kindness which we yield to our parents are called forth by those whom we are accustomed to revere and obey as superiors; but those which we yield to our brothers and sisters are offered to our *equals;* they have more of spontaneous freedom, and, of course, the more aptly prepare us for the society of men, as equals, by forming us to habits of self-command, magnanimity and frankness; by inducing courteous manners, and thus imparting to the social character an aspect of completeness. How finely constituted are some family-circles in relation to this end! Is it not an attractive sight that engages our attention when we behold a brother regarding with a generous and manly pleasure the virtues, the accomplishments, and the happiness of a sister, becoming, as he advances in life, her protector, and her counsellor touching every thing of mutual interest; and, on the other hand, a sister watching with honest pride and joy the expanding character of a brother, hovering around his path like a guardian angel, praying for his success, softening his coarser qualities by the bland influence of her cultivated mind, reproving him for his faults, or rallying him for his follies and vagaries with a good-nature, point, and propriety which lead him to censure himself, yet to love her more, and at last, having become improved in intellect and heart, in habits and manners, acknowledging his debt of gratitude to her for nameless benefits which could have been conferred by no human being unless by one who sustained towards him this benign relationship of sisterhood! Oh, think then how thrice-blessed are these offices of love, and learn to prize this social constitution of the family as a bright display of God's beneficence.

And in following out this rule, let me entreat you to act from *principle* rather than from *impulse*. There are times when the sated savage loses his fierceness, and the blood-stained warrior loves quietness. But this mental state is a mere play of fitful feeling. There is no virtue in it, and it is not trustworthy. The main thing needed to invest our social life with an abiding charm is the schooling of our feelings in subjection to religious principle. This is the only firm foundation of reliable character. On this alone can the fabric of domestic happiness securely rest. And surely, of all our needs on earth, next to that of a peaceful conscience is the need of a peaceful home. We need it as a retreat from the harassing din of earthly cares, and from the sense of dismal solitude that afflicts "the world's tired denizen" amid the icy splendors of heartless society We need it, too, as a place of preparation for a future and a higher state of being. We need this inner realm of life, wherein the finest affections of which the soul is capable may have scope for healthful play and free development. And in order to create and gladden a home like this, Oh, how potent is the true spirit of religion—that love of God which is "the beginning of wisdom!" Where it lives in the heart, it rules with a kingly power, subjects every passion to its sway, and "multiplies grace, mercy, and peace" to all. Under its influence we not only find it easy to be kind on special occasions, but, what is more, we refrain from unkindness amidst ordinary provocations. Wheresoever it hath its way with men, it brings heaven down to earth. Show me a family wherein prevails that fraternal love which "suffereth long and is kind, which envieth not, which vaunteth not itself, is not puffed up, doth not behave itself unseemly, seeketh not her own, is not easily provoked, thinketh no evil," and there my thoughts would fain linger in affinity with the spirit of a scene which the lyres of angels might celebrate as a partial realization of that prophetic song by which they heralded the Messiah's way, breathing "peace on earth and good-will to man."

Having thus called your attention to those duties which the fraternal relation renders especially imperative, let me now, still further, commend to you one or two general maxims that bear directly on that main end which should be kept steadily before the mind in the work of self-improvement:

1. Study day by day to make the faults, weaknesses, or imperfections of your brothers, sisters, and friends minister to the moral elevation of your character. For there is need of care, lest, while we contemplate an ideal standard of social excellence, and while we are pleased with our own conceptions of ideal beauty, we should fail practically of attaining any noble aim

when the daily contrast between that which is ideal and that which is real grates harshly upon the feelings. We may experience a refined mental pleasure in musing upon a lovely picture of domestic life while it glows in all the hues in which a lively fancy may invest it; we may imagine ourselves to be the happy members of a family-circle wherein all the graces of brotherhood and sisterhood are embodied in enchanting forms that we can behold but to love; and yet, when we find it to be our lot to associate with those who have their share of human imperfections, whose faults annoy us, and whose capricious whims, as they may seem to be, balk our best resolves to be kind and amiable, we may be strongly tempted to protect our sensibilities by the rough garb of sullen manners, and by a system of sturdy retaliations. We have seen persons who unconsciously betray this early habitude in various modes of expression; "the show of their countenance doth witness" to this malign bias of their dispositions. This is a great evil. It will sport its ravages within the heart, and blast the finest germs of youthful affections. Guard yourselves against it. Let these infelicities which are, in many cases, incidental to home life, furnish opportunities for the strengthening of character; for overcoming evil with good; for shaming meanness by generosity; for the rectifying of what is wrong by the exemplification of what is right; so shall the petty causes of uneasiness in domestic life develop in you large resources of moral power, become the means of educating the soul to habits of self-command, and of preparing it for glorious triumphs over the sternest difficulties that may afterwards confront it in its earthly career.

2. Above all, let it be remembered that, however strong and fondly-cherished may be the natural ties of brotherhood and sisterhood, they are destined to perish at the touch of death. The most lovely scenes of domestic bliss must soon be covered with a funereal pall. The most happy home that now rings with the laugh of childish glee, or echoes the song of love, must ere long reverberate the melancholy wail that comes from stricken hearts in the hour of separation. In the day of prosperity, when the voice of joy is heard in our dwellings, when blithe and jocund health sparkles in every eye and plays in every feature, when every movement, look, and tone tells of a genial flow of spirits that animates a youthful circle, while it kindles a smile of rapture even on the wan countenance of age, how often does some dim presentiment of sudden change, "casting its shadows before," visit the heart unbidden, and thrill it painfully with strange forebodings! How many have felt the sentiment which was expressed by a loving mother who, on a bright summer evening, standing in the centre of a joyous circle, was congratulated on her happiness, and answered the greeting, with a tear which she sought in vain to conceal, "Oh, this scene is too lovely to last long!" Before a month had passed away, the youngest of that romping group was borne to the cemetery. So fragile are all earthly ties. But the gospel teaches us that there are spiritua bonds which shall outlast even the wreck of nature. The ties of faith and love

that unite true and honest hearts to the Saviour can never be dissolved. His faithful servants, his willing disciples are his real kindred. While he dwelt amongst men, he said of such, These are to me as brothers, sisters and mother: that is, their relation to me combines the sacred endearments of all relations in itself. What a treasure of god-like love is unfolded in that brief saying! Shall it not, then, be your aim to have, "by faith, access into this grace" wherein the Christian stands? Shall it not be yours to answer at once that voice from heaven "which speaketh unto you as unto children," saying, My son, my daughter, "give me thy heart?" Hearken now to this appeal. Consider it well. Let not the illusions of life charm your thoughts away from it. Pray for divine grace, imparted by the Holy Spirit, to aid you effectually, so that you may realize your ideas of truth and duty in immediate action. "To-day, if ye will hear his voice, harden not your heart." Thus, and thus only, can the soul become conscious of benign affections that can never decay; and bearing within itself the assurance of a happy immortality, be gifted with the power to soar, as on eagles' wings, over the ruins of all earthly relationships, to join the brotherhood of kindred spirits in the mansions of the blesse.

Mutual Duties of Householders And Servants.

"THOU SHALT NOT OPPRESS A HIRED SERVANT THAT IS POOR AND NEEDY, WHETHER HE BE OF THY BRETHREN, OR OF THE STRANGERS OF THY LAND WITHIN THY GATES."—Deut. xxiv. 14.

THERE was a large measure of sound sense in the saying of the old Greek, that he would judge of a man's character by the manner in which he treated his servants. The remark, in that case, referred to slaves, who were regarded as property; but the principle involved in it applies with more or less of aptness to our treatment of all those who are inferior to us in point of social position, or in any way dependent upon us for their means of subsistence and enjoyment. For, in our treatment of such persons we *act out ourselves;* we develop the interior and cherished sentiments of our hearts. And certainly, the duties that pertain to the relation of householders and servants, although they do not lay hold of the finer sensibilities of our nature with a grasp so strong as do those which have already engaged our thoughts, yet are they imperative in their claims, are binding on the conscience, are intimately connected with our mental peace and with the prosperity of our families, while they furnish searching tests of our social and Christian character.

The persons who are engaged in domestic service do not appear in the popular theories of society, or in the eyes of the world at large, as occupying stations of commanding influence; yet, regarded as a class, their power for good or evil in the community is immense. What avail the gifts of fortune, the convenient house, or the palatial residence adorned by art and stored with all luxuries of life, if you cannot employ in the routine of daily work the services of those who are competent and trustworthy? When called away from home, what fears must haunt you at every step, if you shall have left your property in the hands of those who are reckless of your interests and have "no fear of God before their eyes!" What anxiety must prey upon a mother's peace if she be obliged to commit her offspring to the care of those whom she believes to be unprincipled or heartless! The most magnificent plans of living, although supported by ample wealth, may be utterly baffled by a failure in the character of domestic servants. They may promote or defeat the best arrangements, and cause the machinery of household affairs to work effectually, or may set it all ajar. If they exemplify the Christian virtues, and exert a healthful influence on the opening minds of the younger children; if they cherish a sympathy with their employers and a concern for their prosperity; if they can be relied on in emergencies; and especially, if in time of sickness and trouble they perform their duties with that readiness and fortitude which spring from a kind nature and religious principle, they are worthy to be prized as among the most precious gifts of Providence; they are entitled to those returns of favor and esteem that shall encourage them in their course of well-doing, and verify to them the words of the poet,

> Honor and shame from no condition rise:
> Act well your part; there all the honor lies.

How important is it, then, that householders consider well their own duties in a relation from which such consequences flow! consequences so closely connected with our character and welfare, not only in this world but in that which is to come. With what beauty and force did the Patriarch Job express his sense of the truth that the Judge of all the earth will cause our conduct towards those engaged in our service to pass in review before his own tribunal, when he exclaimed, (Job xxxi. 13,) "If I did despise the cause of my man-servant or my maid-servant when they contended with me, what shall I do when God riseth up? and when he visiteth, what shall I answer him? Did not he that made me in the womb make them? Did not one fashion us both?" How finely does this strain of ancient poetry illustrate the tendency of true religion to counteract those enmities which too often separate class from class, by awakening in the breasts of all the sentiment of a common obligation to God, and the participation of a common humanity!

I. The FIRST great duty which demands our attention, in regard to those who are engaged in our domestic service, is that which Paul urged on the Christians of his time: that we treat them according to the rule of EQUITY—"giving unto them that which is just and equal." This is simply an enforcement of the golden rule, "Whatsoever ye would that men do unto you, do ye even so unto them." That kind of treatment which reason and conscience tell us we would have just ground to claim if we were in their condition and they in ours, is the treatment which we are bound to observe towards them.

This involves several particulars; and prominent among these is a *fair remuneration for their labor.* To take advantage of their extreme necessities in order to wring out from them those toils which are all the means of sustenance they have, for a stinted pittance that will not suffice with all their efforts to furnish them a decent livelihood, is both unchristian and inhuman. The habits of business which many have formed amidst the strifes of competition, steel their sensibilities against the demands of justice and honor in the financial dealings of domestic life; and a man of wealth who has, when in a favorable mood, contributed large sums to public charities, has been known, on a cold day of winter, to beat down a poor woodsawyer below the regular price, on seeing his eagerness to obtain the job. There are times when one may have the opportunity to deal with all domestics on the same principle; and if this be done, how can faithful service and kind attentions be expected of them?

What wonder if they should feel themselves to be friendless and oppressed, should consider the more favored classes as their enemies, and should nourish in their hearts a sentiment of antipathy? What wonder if it should be found, at last, that such practices have drawn forth fitting retribution from that just Sovereign who said of old by his Prophet, "I will come near to judgment, and will be a swift witness against those that oppress the hireling in his WAGES, the widow and the fatherless, and that turn aside the stranger from his right;" (Malachi iii. 5;) who proclaimed His will at the very commencement of the Jewish Commonwealth, saying, "If thy brother wax poor, and dwell with thee as an hired servant, thou shalt not rule over him with rigor."

And while the divine law insisted on a just reward for labor, it commanded, too, *prompt and regular payment.* With what explicitness and strength of expression it forbade an employer to withhold a poor man's dues a single day after they were wanted! "Thou shalt not oppress a hired servant that is poor and needy, whether he be of thy brethren, or of thy strangers that are in thy land within thy gates. At his day thou shalt give him his hire; neither shall the sun go down upon it: for he is poor, and setteth his heart upon it; lest he cry against thee unto the Lord, and it be sin unto thee." (Deut. xxiv. 14, 15.) Let it be remembered, then, that if a man be careful to preserve his credit with merchants and traders by prompt attention to his payments, the eye of the omniscient Judge is on him for evil if he be dilatory in granting to the poor the reward of labor; and if a lady exhaust her purse in meeting the demands of fashion, or in indulging a taste for luxury and elegance, so as to stint a domestic of her dues, the day will come when the divine warning shall, in some way, be fulfilled: "There shall be sackcloth instead of silk, a sunburnt skin instead of beauty."

In the changing circumstances of a family, it happens not unfrequently that EXTRA WORK is required of one or more in our service; and then the rule of equity demands that *extra pay* be granted. Touching this matter, a domestic may be unreasonably exacting; on the other hand, it is a very bad thing for a man or a woman to be looked upon by any member of the household as being guilty of meanness or extortion—as being ever ready to make large demands on the services of others, and very reluctant to offer a fair recompense. In order to form a just estimate of what is right in all such cases, those whom we employ should be clearly informed as to what are the duties of the station which they are called to fill; they should understand thoroughly, at the outset, what is expected of them. Then, whensoever they may make extraordinary exertions to aid and please the employer, when they go beyond the set limits of the contract, commendation should be bestowed with generous freedom, and their desire to do well should be encouraged by the offer of a meet reward. Yet it has often happened, that seasons of sickness in the family, and the entertainment of company, have exacted from domestics severe and unexpected services that have never received the least acknowledgment. What wonder is it, if, in such cases, their good resolutions pine away for want of aliment! But when it is evident to them that their best efforts are fairly considered, the relation naturally becomes a source of mutual happiness; like that which is spoken of in the New Testament, where it is said, "A certain centurion's servant who was dear unto him was sick and ready to die: and when he heard of Jesus, he sent unto Him the Elders of the Jews, beseeching Him that He would come and heal his servant."

II. This leads me to consider next, the SECOND general duty which devolves on householders in this relation. Besides the law of equity, there is also the "LAW OF KINDNESS" to be observed. This takes within its scope our habits of address, our words and tones, our manners, and the general spirit of our intercourse. All these have their set place among the lights or shadows of home-life; and all these elements of character are comprehended within the reach of that brief precept of the Apostle Paul, which we read in the Epistle to the Ephesians: "*forbearing threatening.*" Every one knows that they who rule well their own houses must have many directions to lay down with great explicitness, many faults to correct, and of course, sometimes, reproofs to administer; but every thing, as to the effect on the mind, depends on the manner and the spirit in which the thing is done. The eyes are the windows of the soul; and if, looking out through them, it dart forth the glance of wrath, contempt or pride, it provokes kindred passions, exasperates where it ought to soothe, and repels where it ought to rule with a gentle influence. Even though, in this way, the point seem to be carried practically, yet it is only for a time. There is gained nothing of that fine control over the mind which gentleness always confers. Undoubtedly, mistakes and errors, faults, follies, and inadvertences will sometimes occur, so as to render a pointed rebuke necessary. Yet, let it be seen that fault-finding is not an agreeable business; that it does not afford you a genial excitement or a pleasant pastime, and that the opportunity is never welcome. "Be ye angry and sin not;" and after the first word of reproof, be especially on your guard; for he who lets passion goad him, punishes himself instead of the offender. What a vivid sense of this truth was expressed by that Grecian philosopher who, being surprised by a friend while standing over a slave with a rod uplifted in his hand, forbearing to strike, was asked what he was doing, and frankly replied, "I am punishing an angry man!"

The law of kindness requires that you cherish an interest in the *health* and *comfort* of those connected with your household service. It must be confessed that employers forget rather too easily that those who labor for them are persons of kindred nature, and have sensibilities as keenly alive to all that constitutes comfort, or discomfort, as are those of the more favored classes. Those of us who have read of the extent to which the boys and girls of the English factories and coal-mines are overworked, have seen a horrible illustration of this tendency; for the poor creatures are forced to toil through hours which ought to be allotted to recreation or repose, until their little muscles lose all their elasticity and tone. Those who urge them to this excess are human beings like ourselves, who began the process with the plea of necessity, then by habit and familiarity became blinded to its shocking evils; and, never having cherished any personal sympathies with the laboring classes, became almost incapable of reasoning aright, touching their own duties towards them. I only allude to this spectacle of misery to indicate the necessity of keeping alive in our bosoms a fellow-feeling with those whom we employ, as human beings, having by nature the same infirmities and wants, the same interior sources of hope and fear, of joy and sorrow, as ourselves. True sympathy is perceptive; it quickens the intellect; it enables us to read human character; without it we cannot understand those with whom we have to do, and are sure to go wrong in our treatment of them. Remembering then, in regard to our domestics, that there is a limit to their power of working and endurance, let us see to it that we avoid making requisitions of them which are inconsistent with the laws of their constitution, or subjecting them to exposures which jeopardize their health, or begrudging to them, when sick, the same medical aid which we would procure for other members of the family. "A righteous man regardeth the life of his beast," saith the Scripture; a kind-hearted farmer abhors the sight of a lean and sickly horse limping uncared for about his premises; much more should one who has the heart of a Christian or a man, provide for the comfort of those who live under his roof, and without whose service his own life would be comfortless.

Of course, then, the law of kindness requires that those who engage in our service should be allowed some time for *recreation*, that they may enjoy a change of scene and opportunities of breathing the fresh air. This is not to be regarded as a mere privilege; it is a demand of absolute necessity; and if some crave it to excess, that can furnish no argument against moderate indulgence. Any regular routine of work that daily tasks the powers of a human being, must be broken now and then by a recreating change, or else the active faculties themselves must soon be broken down. The regular walk, evening and morning, from the kitchen to an attic chamber and from the chamber back to the kitchen, will not suffice to attain the desired end. The mind of every active laborer needs occasionally the exhilarating influence of a change of scene; for it is like the bow—" o'er-bend it, and it breaks."

Moreover, we are bound, in accordance with the law of kindness, to respect the feelings of our domestics, and to protect them against the abuse or insults of children, if any should betray towards them a wanton or a wayward spirit. If they do well in their sphere of duty, it becomes us to speak well of them; and as CHARACTER must be their main dependence, we should readily furnish them with a favorable testimonial, whensoever they may request it, so far as we may be able to do so conscientiously. And if several successive years have witnessed their connection with your family, the faithful performance of their duties, their attention to your interests, their care for your children, their cherished sentiment of identity with your domestic circle, it is not right, in such a case, to dismiss them as mere hirelings, or to allow them to depart from your house without tokens of kind consideration and of sincere desires for their welfare. The law of Moses, alluding to a kind of apprenticeship which existed in Judea, says, "If thy brother, a Hebrew man, or if a Hebrew woman be sold unto thee, and serve thee six years, then in the seventh year thou shalt let him go free from thee. And when thou sendest him out free from thee, thou shalt not let him go away EMPTY. Thou shalt furnish him liberally out of thy flock, and out of thy floor, and out of thy wine-press: of that wherewith the Lord thy God hath given thee, thou shalt give unto him." Mark well the kindly spirit of that old law; six years of faithful service then constituted a peculiar and friendly relation. Would not a similar rule, even in our times, be in accordance with true expediency, with the dictates of humanity and religion? In spite of the general want of fidelity and affection on the part of domestics, in spite of the precariousness of the connection between them and their employers, might not much more be done than has yet been attempted to cultivate what is good in them, to improve their condition, and to make the relation itself more fruitful in tender charities and mutual benefits?

III. The THIRD *general* DUTY which remains to be noticed is this: that we cherish a regard for the spiritual welfare of our domestics. It is doing much for them to remember that they have bodies like our own, and therefore that they have physical wants akin to ours; it is doing more to remember that each one of them has a spiritual and immortal nature. It is a good thing to have a care for their temporal interests; it is a better thing to have a heart to promote those which are spiritual and eternal. "There is no respect of persons with God;" and before Him the soul of a servant is of as much worth as the soul of an emperor. To become the agent of spiritual ruin to an immortal being placed under our guardianship, would be to plait a crown of thorny horrors for our heads in a state of future retribution; to become the voluntary instrument of one's salvation, would be enhancing our happiness on earth and in heaven. Influence is a subtile thing; it is ever streaming from us in manifold directions, and every relation of life which we occupy is a channel through which it flows to attain its end for good or evil. Those who occupy these relations must reap from them harvests of weal or woe; and whether our steps now take hold on the path of life or of death, we shall not go alone, for we are constantly attracting others who will accompany or follow us, 'especially those of our own household." What an interesting moral spectacle is that which enlivens the scenes of social life when the head of a family commands the respect of all whom he employs, and not only their respect as a man, but their confidence as a Christian; when his character radiates its cheering gleam over their path while they are far away from him, so that they are wont to embalm his memory in words of prayer like those which were breathed as sweet incense from the lips of the Patriarch's servant: "O Lord God of my master Abraham, prosper the way which I go!"

In obeying this higher Christian rule of which I speak, to seek the salvation of those who serve us, it becomes us to beware of employing them in any thing which may be "a trap to the conscience." Those who would avoid tempting their children to a dishonest act have been known to have fewer scruples about tempting a servant. Mrs. Opie, in her book on Lying, has illustrated many practices of this sort in her own country. Many of them are too common here. Some persons have tasked their skill to defend the custom of directing a domestic to say at the door, "Not at home," when the lady happened to be engaged, or indisposed to see company, on the ground that the language is *understood.* But whatever pleas of this sort may be gotten up by a fashionable conventionalism, those who are employed to bear such messages understand them only in their simple sense. In the view of domestics, generally, such forms of excuse are falsehoods. With the severity of truth has it been said, "If they consent to lie *for* you, murmur not if they lie *to* you, which they soon will do."

This rule requires, too, that domestics should be allowed, as far as may be possible, the enjoyment of religious privileges, and especially the benefits of the Sabbath. "The Sabbath was made for man;" it was made for *them.* Although works of necessity and mercy are then lawful, it is wrong to demand of our servants any thing that lieth beyond the limit marked by these two terms. If we use the Sabbath as a day of feasting, and, to this end, lay on our domestics heavy tasks, keeping them at home to be engrossed with fatiguing drudgery, we not only wrong our own souls, but we "feast on our servants' birthright." The sacred hours of the Sabbath, beyond the limit already designated, belong to them as their heavenly Father's gift; and if it be treating them unjustly to keep back their *money*, so is it treating them unjustly to deprive them of that *time* which has been set apart for them to employ in laying up that moral treasure which moth and rust cannot corrupt.

Having thus called the attention of householders to those general duties which the Scriptures enjoin on them in relation their domestics, it is proper, now, that I should address a few words to domestics themselves, with the hope that these pages may fall into the hands of some one, or more, of that class of persons.

What though it be true that I am not qualified to advise you by the possession of that practical wisdom that comes from a personal experience of your condition? The Word of God is adapted to the moral wants of men and of women, in every clime and in every station; so that the Christian teacher who heeds its guidance and follows out the lessons which it suggests, by the aid of personal observation, may be perfectly safe in urging its great principles on the minds and hearts of all that are around him, however diversified may be their pursuits, however different from theirs his experience of life may have been. And, as I have pressed on the attention of householders a consideration of the duties which they owe to you, I presume you will unite with me in the statement, that, connected with every obligation which lies upon their consciences in relation to you, there is a correlative duty binding on you in relation to them.

Let us observe the practical application of this general truth in several particulars.

I. The law of EQUITY has claims on you. As soon as you make a definite *engagement* with another, then, for certain considerations, you surrender to their direction that use of your time and your energies which had been previously at your own disposal. Now, the precept of the Scripture which touches this point of your condition is expressed by Paul in his epistle to a young minister, whom that apostle commanded to teach all who are situated in life as you are, that they be careful to "show all good FIDELITY." (Titus ii. 10.)

The law of equity which demands this has respect (1) to property. As far as you are concerned, see that it be not squandered. A man has no moral right to waste his *own* property; much less has any one in his service a moral or a legal right to do so. Be especially on your guard against violating this law, as too many have done, by cloaking a wrong act under the specious name of charity; for some kind-hearted persons have been known to be recklessly extravagant in *secretly* giving away tea, coffee, sugar, and other articles of their employers' property, in order to supply the wants of the poor! What an immense amount of property has thus gone out from a low window, or a back-door, without ever having been accounted for! And some who have habitually done this thing have been unwilling to admit even to themselves that it was criminal, because, forsooth, it was the excuse of charity. When such a process of varnishing over the act of "purloining" by specious names has been once commenced, it will seldom cease until it shall have developed its nature in some deed of startling crime that will bring with it the blight of inward peace and the ruin of reputation.

(2) This rule, too, relates to the disposal of *time.* For "time is money;" and a careless loiterer will consume much wealth in the course of a year by baffling every arrangement which may have depended on his or her punctuality. It is in exact accordance with the spirit of this remark that Paul lays it down so explicitly as a rule for Christian servants, that they should so clearly act from a right principle as that they should not need constant watching. He charges it upon them that they should attend to their work, "not with eye-service as men-pleasers, but as the servants of Christ, doing the will of God from the heart." (Ephes. vi. 6.) The old proverb, "punctuality is the life of business," applies as well to the business of the household as to that of the market or exchange; and it is equally true in the one place as in the other, that "he that is slothful is brother to him that is a great waster."

(3) This rule also relates to reputation. It is in the power of almost every domestic to do immense injury to the peace and welfare of a family by a careless repetition of remarks which may have been overheard, or by parading before the gaze of idle curiosity

all the trifling incidents and the unhappy difficulties which may occur to one's view within the interior circle of home-life. This course of conduct is sinful: it is directly forbidden by the Scripture. The apostle Paul severely condemns the social habits indulged by those women who, as he says, "learn to be idle, wandering about from house to house; and not only idle, but TATTLERS also and busybodies, speaking things which they ought not." (1 Tim. v. 13.) Abuse no advantage of your position in a family to display those faults and troubles which a Christian spirit would lead you to veil rather than expose.

II. Let me urge you to observe again, that beyond the law of equity, there is another law which has claims on you; namely, the *law of kindness.*

In the course of events which pertain to the history of every family, unexpected difficulties will arise—sudden emergencies, which no human wisdom could have foreseen. Disappointment and trouble will come in some form; neither rank, wealth, nor power, can keep them at bay. Resolve, I pray you, to share these difficulties with your employer. Do not forsake an afflicted family. Be ever ready to lend them a helping hand in time of trouble. Do not be afraid to strain a nerve, now and then, to render their passage over the rough places of life's pathway as easy as possible.

In regard to this point of which I am speaking, there may be seen some very strange contrasts in the conduct of persons engaged in domestic service. There are those who seem to be ever ready to perform an act of kindness; their patience "never faileth;" they are never "put out," and, as the saying is, "you always know where to find them." Others, again, are so peevish as to fret about every petty trouble, and they are able, by their sullen looks and tones of voice, to keep all that are around them in a state of nervous uneasiness. The want of some convenience about the house or kitchen that may have been seen somewhere else, the arrival of a visitor having a claim on the family's hospitality, an unexpected number of guests at dinner, or the entrance of sudden sickness into the household—these, one or more, with other nameless disturbances which are incidental to this mortal state, have been found sufficient to keep the minds of some domestics for ever agitated, and have caused them as much feverish excitement as would properly arise from the dread of overwhelming calamities. Is not the indulgence of such a temper a foolish waste of the energies of life? Undoubtedly; yet it is very common. If your weaknesses lie in this direction, fail not to pray for divine grace and wisdom to aid you in getting the better of them. Wheresoever such malign dispositions are allowed to have their way, they prey upon the soul like a fell disease, and invest the whole character with a mean and disgusting aspect.

I would commend these latter suggestions, especially, to the notice of those members of the Church who are engaged in domestic service. We see, from the writings of the Apostle Paul, how desirous he was that they who are pursuing this walk of life should illustrate true religion by example, or, as he expresses it, (Titus ii. 10,) "that they may adorn the doctrine of

God our Saviour in all things." It has sometimes been seen, that the influence of a faithful servant has revolutionized the moral condition of a whole family; and a blessed achievement like this graced the humble history of one who sustained this relation, respecting whom a wealthy lady was heard to say, "That girl has done more for me and for my household than any friend that I have in this world." What a fine testimonial of Christian excellence! The name of "that girl" is unknown to fame; but when God's faithful ones shall be gathered at his bidding, her character shall shine in celestial beauty; for of such as these it is written, "They shall be mine, saith the Lord, in the day when I make up my jewels."

III. Hence, I am led to observe, that it is your duty to act habitually from *a supreme regard to your own everlasting salvation*, and to *the spiritual good of all the household* with which you are connected. This suggestion accords with the spirit of our Saviour's advice to all of us: "Seek ye first God's kingdom and His righteousness, and all things else shall be added unto you."

If this advice deserve any regard at all, it deserves *supreme* regard. If it be worth any thing, it is worth every thing. And there is need of a special effort of the mind to lay it well to heart, so as to carry it out in action. For, at the outset of any course of business which necessity compels us to pursue, one object of thought naturally engages the whole attention; that object is *success.* All the faculties of the soul become engrossed in providing for the wants of the body. In this way, how easily we become forgetful of the momentous fact, that we inherit an immortal nature; that what men call *death*, is but the release of the spirit from its imprisonment in a house of clay; that then, having entered upon a new career, its faculties must be for ever expanding, and its desires after real good for ever increasing in scope and intensity. In this connection, I have often thought what a weight of meaning was enfolded in those few words which the patriarch Abraham addressed to a departed spirit in another state of being: "Son, remember that thou in thy *lifetime* receivedst thy good things!"

As the soul cannot be satisfied with earthly things, it must have spiritual sustenance adapted to its nature. Hence, our Saviour declared, repeating the words of Moses, "Man shall not live by *bread* alone, but by every *word* that proceedeth out of the mouth of God shall man live." The truth of God's Word—this is the proper aliment of the immortal spirit. Whosoever neglects this "bread of Heaven," may care well for the body, but he starves the soul.

Allow me therefore to urge upon your attention two or three important rules of action.

(1.) Make the Bible your daily companion. It will be your safeguard in hours of temptation, your solace in trouble, a friendly counsellor amidst scenes of prosperity. You may be heavily pressed with the cares of life, you may be harassed day by day by the pressure of your business urging you forward in the excitement of a constant hurry; nevertheless, do not allow yourself for these reasons to become estranged from your Bible. Be faithful to it in spite of them. If you cannot read much, do not, on that account, forbear to read a little. A single sentence, a single line may come suddenly to remembrance amidst the din of rasping cares, like a message fresh from heaven, diffusing through the heart a balmy influence, and soothing an agitated mind into contentment and peace.

(2.) As far as may be possible, use the Sabbath as a means of spiritual benefit. Do not permit yourself to be utterly deprived of this inestimable blessing. It is proper that, in every new engagement, you should stipulate for a reasonable allowance of time on the Sabbath, so that you may be able to attend the services of the sanctuary once, at least, during the day. Having secured this privilege, guard against every temptation to waste these hallowed hours in dissipating amusements, in idle gossip, or needless visitation.

(3.) Under the guidance of the Scriptures, let it be your aim to live a truly Christian life. Let your intercourse with others, and your whole deportment, be such that you shall be able *to respect yourself.* Let it be made evident that, "as far as in you lieth," your own religious character is a reality, and that it is your great endeavor to preserve it untarnished, in its simplicity and its purity. Thus it will be clearly shown not only that you respect yourself, but that you have *reason* to do so; and so shall you constrain others to respect you, even though it may be against their inclination. The pride of rank and the pride of wealth, connected with conscious meanness or wickedness, will sometimes cower before the bright example of one far below them in point of worldly position; just as it happens, now and then, that

> — haughtiest princes veil their eyes
> Before the poorest slave.

If your path through the world, thus far, has been rough and gloomy; if you have had to contend with disheartening difficulties, with orphanage, with the desertion of friends, with poverty, with varied forms of calamity, yet, by the power of character formed on those principles which are taught in the New Testament, you may rise superior to all these outward evils, and stand upright in a real dignity of soul, in the strength of a serene conscience, and in favor both with God and man.

Let it not be thought by any reader that the preceding remarks and rules have been culled from books; and that, though they " may do well enough in a sermon," they are not really practicable " as the world now is." In this discourse, there is not a principle, a rule, or a suggestion, which I have not seen realized in action; and so realized as to adorn and cheer the scenes of home-life. They are all, I think, in harmony with the teachings and the spirit of Christianity as set forth in those four Gospels which contain the biogragraphy of our Saviour. When these teachings of our Master shall have shed their light over all the nations, when their spirit shall have modified the public sentiment of every community, when families shall have grown up under their benign influence, then, and not till then, shall the long-desired social renovation of mankind have been accomplished. Then every house shall be a *home*. Then the affections of every heart shall find a sphere of healthful play within the household circle. Then the war of classes shall have well-nigh ceased. Then "the lion and the lamb shall lie down together." Then it shall be seen that the finest fruits of Christian civilization are not to be found in the triumphs of art, in the increase of material comforts, in the subjugation of rude nature to the dominion of mind, but rather in the production of noble and reliable CHARACTER; in the rearing of self-governed men and women, who shall develop in all the social relations those elements of character which constitute true goodness, true greatness, and true happiness.

Duties of Principals to Clerks and Apprentices.

"HAPPY ARE THY MEN, HAPPY ARE THESE THY SERVANTS."—
1 Kings x. 8.

THE well-being of every community depends essentially on a spirit of mutual confidence, and of friendship, sincerely cherished by the different classes of persons who compose it. In saying this, we only state a general law which shines by its own light. And when we consider that the men who now occupy the various posts of business within the realm of commerce or mechanic art, and those youth whom they are training up to take their places, or to make new ones for themselves, constitute the very life and strength of the commonwealth, we cannot but see how desirable and how necessary it is, that the relation between them should be one of amity and kindness; that while, on the one hand, the clerk and the apprentice should be benefited by the wisdom and skill of the employer, on the other hand, he should find in them those qualities of aptness, diligence, and fidelity, which will render their services valuable to him. It is only a widespread relationship of this sort that can lay a solid basis for social order and permanent prosperity. If, on the part of the employer, there be indulged a prevailing spirit of rapacity, selfishness, or indifference, and on the part of his young men an utter disregard of his interests, or a vengeful sentiment of retaliation, the scenes of business become a school for the education of the worst and meanest passions; a miserable place of preparation for the duties of the present life, and still less adapted to prepare one for the allotments of "the life to come." Nevertheless, whosoever will take manly views of both the present and the future, resolving at the outset to render this relation friendly, parental, confidential, giving scope to generous feelings and to Christian aims, will find, in the peculiar duties which pertain to it, deep springs of mental satisfaction and delight.

But the question arises, What are these duties? what is their extent? There are many who have never considered them at all; and many who deny their obligation. "I know of no peculiar duties that I owe to a clerk or apprentice," once said an employer who was all-engrossed in the pursuits of business; "they come to me in order to earn a livelihood, and as long as they behave well, I treat them civilly, as I would all others with whom I have any thing to do." But could he thus easily discard all the moral obligations arising from his particular connection with them? Would his Maker and Judge ratify such a disclaimer as that?

Does not every new relationship into which we enter give rise to some new, specific duty, and bring upon us a corresponding responsibility? In one of the most instructive parables that was ever uttered, our Saviour tells us of two men, professedly religious, who, travelling from Jerusalem to Jericho, saw by the wayside a poor sufferer, who had been attacked and robbed; as there he lay in his blood, his wounds appealed "with their dumb mouths" to the heart of humanity: but they looked coldly on the scene, disclaimed all responsibility, and passed on their journey. They had harmed no one, and could gravely say that they did not feel bound to repair the injuries which others had committed. But did Heaven hold them guiltless? The very fact that they were brought nigh a fellow-man whose necessities made him dependent on them for special aids which they had the power to confer, rendered him in a legal sense their *neighbor*, because it brought him within the scope of that command of God which bids us "love our neighbor as ourselves," or, in other words, to make his happiness our own. The picture which our Lord has drawn to illustrate the spirit of that precept, presents a touching case of bodily suffering; yet, are there not *moral* needs, wants of the mind and heart, as urgent as any that are felt by flesh and sense? Are there not wounds of the spirit to be healed? Are there not those around you whose dependent and exposed condition pleads for them that you would pour in upon their souls "the oil and wine" of kindness, counsel, and a healthful moral influence?

If it be a binding duty on us to "do good unto all

men as we have opportunity," have not those youth who are in daily association with their seniors for the purpose of learning to manage the business of life, high claims on their employers for the exercise of sympathy, care, and friendly vigilance, simply because there is no class of human beings, beyond the precincts of one's own family, who furnish so many opportunities of conferring needed benefits?

Inquiries like these, when fairly set in the light of Christian principles, admit only of an affirmative answer. Let us proceed, then, to consider the moral duties which belong to the relation of the employer and the employed; and, FIRST, the duties which devolve on the employer.

I. PRIMARILY, it becomes all those who have youth under their care, for purposes of business, to allow them every practicable advantage which they may need, in order to acquire an *adequate knowledge of their calling.* As a public teacher of youth, when his scholars are about to pass an examination in the school-room or the counting-room, feels a deep concern that they should be well qualified in the branches which have engaged their attention, so every man of business should cherish the desire that those young men who go forth from his establishment should have a competent knowledge of their profession. Indeed, the word "apprentice" originally meant a scholar, being derived from the French verb *apprendre*—to learn; and although the word *university* is now confined to an institution of science and literature, in old times it was the name given to an incorporated body of business men; so that they used to speak of "the university of smiths," "the university of clothiers," and would also apply the word to other combinations. And certainly, he who considers the welfare of his country, will see it to be as important that the young men who graduate from farms, shops, and counting-rooms, should be qualified for their pursuits, as that those who graduate at a college should know as much as their diplomas certify. If all the institutions of learning in the land should turn out poor scholars, no one, in particular, might take any blame to himself; yet, what an amount of calamity and dishonor would this course bring upon the nation! How difficult would it become to find men qualified for the bench and the bar, the medical chair, the sick-room, or the pulpit! Not less would our national character suffer, if "the universities of trades" should send forth young men deficient in elementary knowledge. So important was this matter deemed in France, so long ago as the last century, that there proper officers were appointed to examine a young man ere he was allowed to set up in business as an educated apprentice; and if he were engaged in any department of the arts, he was required to bring before them a fair specimen of his work. If he succeeded, he was called an aspirant, or a candidate for mastership. This arrangement had a powerful influence in elevating professional character in all branches of business, and thus, in promoting the national interests. Although, in this country, the government could not carry such a plan as this into effect, yet the great end which it aimed at is as important here as elsewhere; the attainment of it, however must be left to that public opinion which gives law to custom. Evidently, therefore, a patriotic spirit—a regard to the common welfare, as well as a sense of duty to God, and of justice to the inexperienced youth —should urge every head of an establishment to see to it that all who are under his care attain that knowledge of their duties which will qualify them to "teach others also," to sustain well their position as members of society, and to honor that calling to which they devote their lives.

Obvious facts give moral force to these considerations. Too often have we seen that the young man who enters upon the arena of business without an efficient preparation, has been, on that account, pressed with responsibilities which he could not bear—surrounded with difficulties with which he had not power to cope; and then, when disaster had long tracked his steps, and utter failure had disheartened him, he has sought relief from trouble in the wine-cup—has formed habits of dissipation whose chains he could not break, and has sunk down, helpless and hopeless, "a dead weight" upon the community.

II. But besides imparting to young men that kind of education which consists in knowledge and skill, it becomes those who are masters in business, by both precept and example, *to train up all who are under their care to honorable habits of business.*

I use the term "honorable" in a sense that befits the lips of a Christian, as opposed to every thing dishonest, mean, and deceitful. It is said that "there is honor among thieves;" and he who admits no higher standard of honor than the prevailing social law, may sometimes place the stamp of honor on infamy itself. But in a truly civilized and Christian community, no one can habitually violate the law of equity, can direct his dependants to tell lies for a profit, or pursue a course of dealing which requires him to creep like a serpent, instead of moving erect like a man, without destroying his self-respect, making an enemy of his own conscience, nor without feeling some disgust for a pursuit whose gains must be gotten by so enormous a sacrifice. Dishonesty is dishonor; and far better would it be that commerce should languish, or be managed on the narrow scale of the patriarchal ages, than that the moral sense, the honor, the integrity of the nation, should be laid as a whole burnt-offering on its shrine.

But this is not necessary. Commerce is a want of society, and may be conducted on honorable principles Were it otherwise; were it true, as some have thought, that "every trade must have its tricks," and that the moral law of veracity, though excellent in theory, cannot be applied in practice, what would this prove, but that all commercial business is contrary to nature, and a conspiracy against the government of God? Let him who speaks in this way establish his proposition, and what has he done, but shown that all the arrangements of mercantile life are at war with public virtue, with the ingenuous character of youth, with our national welfare, as well as the laws of Heaven; and that it is the duty of every friend of religion and humanity, of the mother who breathes her gentle teachings in the nursery to the boy whose moral health she values more than life, and of the minister in the sanctuary who commends to the divine keeping the interests of his country, to pray that the Almighty would blast the whole system by the thunders of his power, rather than to ask that he would foster our commerce by his providential care? What has he done, but given reason to expect the working out of such a ruin under the government of a Being who "hateth iniquity," who "taketh up the isles as a very little thing," to whom "the nations are but as the small dust of the balance," and who will not much regard the number of our ships which whiten every sea, or the strength of our lofty storehouses which beautify our cities, or the grandeur of our merchants' palaces, adorned with unjust gains, but will lay them all under the ban of his wrath when "the day of visitation" cometh, in the exercise of the same high sovereignty as was expressed in the doom pronounced against Jerusalem—"Take away her battlements, for they are not the Lord's!"

We affirm again our belief that falsehood is not necessary in the business of life; and, being friends of commerce, would assert its moral dignity as the great agent in the civilization of the world and the progress of society. One great reason why a departure from integrity has seemed, in the view of many, to be so necessary and so politic, and why the avowal of it has become so much more popular in our time than it was formerly, is, that there has been more deeply cherished a ruling passion for the quick acquisition of fortune, and for a certain extravagant style of life. It is true, human nature has not changed; but the boundless realm of speculation, which was opened in this country some few years ago, has nourished this passion to strange excess. And when passion rules, the mind is blind; for no more than the bat can it see things truly by daylight. While under its spell, moral considerations are not treated as realities, and the soul becomes reckless of the means by which the end is gained. There is a dimness of moral perception; the sensibility to evil is blunted. Even now, we are not affected by deviations from honorable dealing as our fathers would have been; crimes which would have shocked them profoundly, scarcely ruffle the surface of our self-complacency. If a man only get a fortune, no matter how, too often his success is his defence; its glitter hides the odiousness of the means. He who steals a dollar is charged with larceny, and is called a criminal; he who, by an ingenious process, abstracts thousands from an insurance company or a mercantile firm, is called by the softer name of a "defaulter," and commands respect in some sort, according to the boldness of his operation. The love of party triumph invented the saying, "All's fair in politics;" and if the phrase, "All's fair in trade," is not uttered as a popular maxim, a large class of facts might be cited to show that by many it has been practically adopted. Deception in small things is connived at, until, at last, utter recklessness becomes the disease of a community. To what ultimate results these things have tended, and would have reached had they been left unarrested by the hand of Providence, we can easily guess, when we remember that several leading statesmen have boldly advocated the policy of repudiating debts which it is not convenient to pay, have seen themselves sustained by large parties in the States where they live, and have thus turned the eyes of foreign nations away from the misfortunes of our land, to behold with astonishment the vast extent to which there has obtained a dereliction from principle.

One of the imperative duties, therefore, which men of business owe to the youth around them, is, to cherish in their breasts a manly sentiment in favor of honorable dealing. Let them be "rooted and grounded" in the truth, that it is no disgrace to become the victims of poverty, to be conquered by misfortunes which could not be foreseen; but that for them, though encouraged by the example of others, to strike out bold schemes of business, and to calculate on bringing matters to a crisis, so as to pay "thirty-three cents on a dollar," is to act on a principle which not only involves sin and shame, but, in its issues, brings the judgments of God on the individual, and temporal ruin on the community. Let their integrity be held sacred. Let fair dealing be made a point of honor, and let them be taught that, if men understand their profession as merchants, they can manage the business of exchange between the producer and the consumer, with advantage to all, without the help of fraud and chicanery.

III. It is the duty of the employer to furnish to the youth under his care those *moral aids* which will enable them to cope with the peculiar temptations that beset them. Every young man, especially in a great city, is called to a stern moral conflict with the leagued hosts of evil—a battle which is in constant progress, and in which, now and then, there comes a critical moment whereon his destiny is suspended. A slight incident will sometimes become the turning-point of a history. In The London Illustrated Magazine is a story entitled "Life behind the Counter," which was intended to show, by a vivid picture, how entirely the complexion of a young man's character was determined by a conversation which led him to forego a concert and a supper with a company who were inclined to dissipation, in order to enjoy a walk and the society of an excellent friend. This representation is true to nature; for often, with some such trivial event, comes that great question of life and death, which, in some way or other, comes to every man—that question which a Greek mythologist would express by the startling phrase, "Will you join the dragons or the gods?" Not a day passes without verifying this statement; for where is the young man who is not obliged to consider invitations which, if accepted, will give a new turn to his thoughts, a new character to his company, and affect the whole atmosphere of moral influence which he will afterwards inhale?

Now, in order that he may safely meet these exigencies, he needs, as the first and greatest aid which an employer can do somewhat to bestow, a well-spent SABBATH. "The Sabbath was made for man" by Him who made man, who understood his constitution and his wants. It is a heritage for all—a birthright which God has given to every one. He has shown his regard to our *physical* wants in the varied gifts of nature so freely lavished on us; and the addition of the Sabbath to all these attests his paternal care for the culture of that immortal spirit which is destined to rise from the ruins of the body to a full development of its powers, in a course of eternal progression. He has engraven the Sabbath-law, not only on the stone tables of the decalogue, but on the very frame-work of the human race; for, just as, by observing the alternation of day and night, we see that the principle of *rest*, as well as of *action*, is a part of the system of the universe, so, by noticing the different effects of the observance or violation of the Sabbath on the health, strength, and life of active men, (and indeed of all working animals,) we see that the seventh-day rest, as well as the night rest, is a part of this same system. Man, borne along by the vigor of his mind, does not show the physical effect of this constant diurnal exertion so soon as the laboring brute, but breaks down at last more suddenly: as is observed particularly by Dr. Combe, in his book on health, where he names several public men, who, acting under the influence of "ambition, or natural eagerness of mind, have been suddenly arrested in their career by the inordinate action of the brain, induced by incessant toil." Yet, although the voice of nature unites with the voice of revelation, in the utterance of the command, "Remember the Sabbath-day, to hallow it," the chief benefit of the Sabbath is not physical, but moral and religious. It is designed as a counterpoise to those mighty influences of every-day life which tend to make the soul the slave of sense and passion—those influences of which, in their relation to youth, the poet Burns has sung so plaintively:—

"Alternate follies take the sway,
Licentious passions burn:
This, tenfold force gives Nature's law,
That man was made to mourn."

In order to counteract this tendency of the soul to become the victim of low sensuality, to instruct and quicken the conscience, to cultivate a taste for sober truth, to emancipate and exalt the spiritual nature, a Sabbath is needed by mankind; and the institution accomplishes these ends by its involving the acknowledgment of our relation to the divine Lawgiver, by strengthening a sense of accountability to him, calling off the mind from the visible to the invisible, from the temporal to the eternal, and by turning the attention to those momentous revelations which he has addressed to us in his holy Word. It is a means of improvement which cannot be neglected with impunity. As every violated law of nature will avenge itself, so will Sabbath-breaking be followed by special penalties; and thousands of instances prove that the very FIRST STEP in that course of youthful determination which ends in the wreck of character and happiness, has been the desecration of the Sabbath.

Undoubtedly, a calm survey of things in our great cities will convince any one that there is very little danger of exaggerating the importance of the Sabbath in its relation to young men; for many of those who have deeply fallen, in retracing their history have fixed on certain eras of its course, have been led to confess that some riding or sailing-party, some refectory, or bar-room, or idle company associated with Sabbath-dissipation, marks the sharp turning-point of life's downward path, and that the retrospect forces them to say with poor Gibbs, who suffered death for crime, "But for the violation of the Sabbath, I might have been a good and happy man."

And in view of such a class of facts, may we not fairly appeal to employers with the question, whether it is not probable that some of the young men within the sphere of their influence will reap from their Sabbath-violations such wretched harvests as these persons bewailed too late? Any one who has had occasion to pass a Sabbath in the vicinity of a large city like New York or Boston, has probably been struck with scenes which must give to this inquiry a painful significance. At Hoboken, or at Chelsea, for instance, during some seasons of the year, what throngs of youth may be seen riding to places of low resort, to spent the day in drinking, gaming, and revelry; and then again returning to the city under the maddening excitement of their sports and cups, pouring forth profanity in their unseemly conversation and their songs, while their looks, tones, and manners, show that they glory in their recklessness! Some of them, doubtless, are the sons of rich men, without employment; but most of them are clerks or apprentices, who can ill afford the mere waste of money thus incurred, and who are encircling themselves with the most potent temptations to leap over the bounds of honesty, and to take by stealth the means of their demoralizing pleasures. And withal, there is great reason to fear that many of them have passed through the initiating process, and have become hardened in the worst of habits, without having felt the power of *one earnest effort on the part of their employers* to learn what was actually going on in the shaping of their destinies, or to win them over to a right moral and religious observance of the Sabbath. And surely, seeing that in all these cases the perverted blessing becomes a curse, that the medicine misused is turned into a poison, how carefully should an employer guard against trespassing on a young man's Sabbath, or tempting any one under his influence to part with it for love or for money.

2. Another moral aid which an employer may confer on a young man, is the *expression of a personal interest in his welfare*, by means of such friendly suggestions as may rouse him to resist temptation, and to cherish high aims in the pursuit of life. We could easily mention instances where a single word of caution has been attended with a long train of happy consequences. For, sometimes the power of temptation is unsuspected, and the first yielding to it comes of inadvertence. The demon hides his cloven foot while smiles wreathe his features, and his lips distil honeyed words. Thus it was in the case of an ingenuous and confiding young salesman, who, at the age of twenty-one, was fatally injured by the company he happened to meet at a restaurant. At first he had resorted thither merely to save his time, and the necessity of a long walk in obtaining his meals. No doubt, his eye had been attracted by the choice birds displayed at the door, and by the tasteful arrangement of the show-window He had noticed there several times a young

man somewhat older than himself, who one day addressed him by inviting him to enjoy a very fine cigar, from a box imported by a friend. The invitation was accepted. Next followed a proposal to step into an adjoining billiard-room where several were engaged in playing for money. "Let's watch the progress of the game," said his new acquaintance. Having assented to this, in a few moments he became *deeply interested.* Ere long, he was asked to try himself, for a small sum. Nothwithstanding his want of practice, his hand, his eye, and aim, and steadiness of nerve, were praised. To his own astonishment, he succeeded; for there are places where novices are always allowed to succeed in their first efforts. Then came the soft insinuation, "It is easy for you to win!" This was a *new idea.* Its effect was electrical. A new charm invested the terrible amusement, and his whole mental energy became absorbed in its pursuit. He soon sought deeper and deeper play; dollar after dollar was won, the routine of his business became tedious and distasteful, and in due time his experienced and skilful tempter, in one fatal hour, swept from him all he possessed, and left him ruined as to his purse, his peace of mind, and a reputation more precious than gold. What a wreck of character and happiness was this! And yet it might have been prevented by the timely hint that would have led him to spend in a better place that noonday hour when his unguarded feet first trod the path of the Destroyer.

3. Another mode in which an employer may afford moral aid to a young man, is to furnish him *incentives*

to occupy his hours of leisure usefully, so that by means of books and associations for the pursuit of knowledge he may find scope for his love of excitement. For here we have named a mighty element of temptation—this love of excitement which glows in every human bosom, which, in its intenser actings, has set one adrift from home to roam the ocean, lured by the romance of a sailor's life; has impelled another to court hardships in travelling over continents and mingling with foreign nations; has led a third to abandon the retreat of quiet affluence in order to embark his capital in commercial enterprise; which was in an ancient age the soul of war, of chivalry and crusades, and is now the spring of that activity which is turning the Western forest into a garden, peopling the golden soil of California with Northern youth, and disturbing the haunts of the savage with the whiz of the steam-car or the hum of the factory. Now he who is at the head of an establishment in business, finds scope and play for this love of excitement in managing his affairs, in grappling with difficulties, and in his forecast for the future. In this, however, the clerk or the apprentice does not participate. He goes through the routine of his duties, perhaps becomes jaded with them for want of a genial interest, and then where shall he find the mental excitement which he craves? It is this desire which lays his soul open to the worst of snares. One fact stated in a public document speaks volumes on this subject. It was in evidence before the grand jury in Boston, some time ago, that one of the city police officers, on a Saturday night in November, during a walk of less than a mile in extent, passed more than one hundred persons, mostly young men, in a state of partial or entire intoxication! Had these all fallen on a Mexican battle-field, the whole country would have mourned their loss. Had their corpses been brought home for burial, the city would have been clad in funeral drapery, and the sad array would have awakened in every breast those deep emotions which no words, or plaintive music, or outward signs of grief, could adequately express. Yet here were the evidences of a more tremendous ruin, exciting in the hearts of mothers and sisters a keener sorrow which no voice of public sympathy could soothe, and calling forth tears the more bitter because they were shed only in silent solitude.

The commencement of such a career is easy—the return difficult, though not impossible. Oh for the prevention—the prevention! This is worth more than the cure. And what is this? It is to guard against the *first steps*. It is to surround the young mind with counteracting influences and good associations. It is to have an eye and a heart for the welfare of those under your care when they are away from you, instead of verifying the proverb, "Out of sight, out of mind." It is to appeal to them by all the power of personal address and by all the worth of your friendship. It is to arouse in them a desire for self-improvement—a preference for those associations of which mental culture is the object; to quicken within them the love of knowledge, and, by encouraging their hopes of success in business, to stimulate their minds with an excitement like that which imparts to your own a degree of tone and energy. If, in the city, they are at a distance from their early homes, it is to find a place for them as much like a home as possible, and not leave them to form their first acquaintanceships amidst the chance-company of a boarding-house, of which neither knows the character. It is to open to them the path to such society as will meet the demands of their social nature, from its adaptation to both please and profit them: for it has often happened that a young man's acquaintanceship with a single family has become the great *conservative power* of his character, the guiding-star in his moral firmament, shedding its benignant rays over that trackless deep on which he has been tossed in succeeding years.

Above all, it is imperatively necessary to favor every influence which shall tend to build up character on the foundation of religious principle. This is a solid and enduring basis. "The fear of the Lord is the beginning of wisdom." Without this source of strength, there can be but slight grounds of trust that any human character will withstand the assaults of temptation. Intellectual culture and good social influences may do much to form correct tastes and sound morals; but there are trials wherein the soul needs stronger defences than these can furnish — trials in which those maxims, resolutions, and habits, which sufficed in ordinary times, become like battlements of wood before a spreading flame. It is only character, with whose interior elements religious principle is so thoroughly incorporated as to form a part of its very substance, that can come forth from the fires of temptation, like golden ore from the furnace, purified from dross and increased in value.

It is not likely that these pages will fall into the hands of any employer who would not be glad, if he had the opportunity, to put forth an effort in behalf of any one of his young men, in order to save a large earthly fortune from threatened ruin. But how much greater will be the joy in the retrospect of life, of having aided effectually to secure to them a treasure which no thief can steal, no calamity destroy; lasting as eternity, and more precious than a thousand worlds!

Duties of Young Men to their Employers.

"THOU HAST BEEN FAITHFUL OVER A FEW THINGS, I WILL MAKE THEE RULER OVER MANY THINGS."—Matt. xxv. 21.

HAVING called the attention of employers to some of those imperative duties which relate to the young men under their care, we would now address a few considerations to those young men themselves, who have entered into the relations which they hold to their employers in order to become prepared for their chosen pursuits. These have reached the most critical period of life. There is an obvious reason why the season of clerkship or apprenticeship should be so regarded. It belongs to the portion of time devoted to preparation for the duties and cares of a profession, for the toils and the struggles by which each is to work out the problem that involves his own failure or success; and of that preparation it is the *closing period.* If in earlier days much time has been lost, there is yet some chance for redeeming it; if mistakes have been made, they may now in a great degree be rectified.

We have sometimes seen that those who have been negligent of study while at school, and even indolent in their habits, have been transformed into all that was active and promising when called to live and move amidst the stirring scenes of business. A sense of necessity sharpened their faculties; then, a consciousness of power stimulated them to exertion, and at last, a real delight in their work became a spring of constant and successful activity. But if this probation be passed without due improvement, if a young man fail to gain a thorough knowledge of his calling, if by yielding to temptation he dissipates his time and money, and thus forms habits adverse to a life of business, it is almost impossible to remedy the evil; he starts on the career of manhood quite unfitted for the race, moves ever with a faltering or a tardy step, and, in the end, falls short of the goal that shone before him when "distance lent enchantment to the view."

I. The first important duty with which a young person should charge himself on entering the establishment of his employer, is to fix his attention on *the true object of the relation* which has then begun to exist. Many have become awake to it just when it was too late for their minds to feel its quickening influence, and only in time to regret that they had not seen it before. As many a student, when about to bid farewell to the university, has expressed his astonishment that four years of his life had flown so rapidly away, and also the wish that he could roll back the wheels of time, and pass over the course again with a true sense of the great end and aim before him, so, many a young man of business, as he stepped forth from beneath the roof of protection and guardianship to "set up for himself," to take his place on the arena of competition, where he would have to cope with the strong and the experienced, has felt for the first time the responsibility of his position, and has seen the worth of that preparatory training which alone could qualify him to grapple with the difficulties, to break the snares, and escape the perils that beset him. Let him, therefore, early apprehend the truth that apprenticeship is no mere formality; that its design is not merely to teach the theory of a business, or to show him the things to be done, or how to do them, but to endow him with that power which comes from a HABIT of doing them. The "second nature" formed by habit must be one secret of his success. From this come aptness and skill. When you observe an attendant in a store wrapping a piece of goods with neatness and despatch, it seems easily done; yet even that could not be well imitated by an untutored hand without repeated trials It is not enough to see another do it; there must be the training of practice. It is so in every thing that may be called professional. Whether you look upon the sailor who seems to feel as much at home upon the "high and giddy mast" as does a bird upon the bough, or the musician who sweeps all the chords of his instrument as with a magic touch, and without the appearance of an effort, or the officer of the bank who counts vast sums of money with electrical rapidity and with the coolest confidence, or the accountant whose books display the mazes of a complicated business with a beautiful regularity that gives his work the aspect of an amusement more than of a task, reflection teaches you that nothing of this could be accomplished without a close attention and a long practice which have educated the mind to quickness, and every muscle and nerve to obedience. But then the acquisition is worth the cost. To be a thorough master of one's business adds immensely to his enjoyment and usefulness in life. At the outset, therefore, of an engagement with an employer, it is well to be resolved on watching against every temptation to form lax and careless habits, to be a loiterer, to do things out of their proper time, or to yield to those amusements which check the growth of an energetic interest in your chosen employment. Adopt the maxim of Paul, "not slothful in business;" even though to carry it out may require self-denial and discipline. It will lead to success; for "seest thou a man diligent in his business? He shall not stand before mean men; he shall stand before kings, and not be ashamed."

II. In subordination to this rule, is another still more particular, the adoption of which has been productive of good effects: this is, *conform yourself to all the regulations of the establishment.* It was a wise saying of the old Persians, that no man is fit to command who has not learned to obey. The discipline of their public schools, as exhibited by Xenophon, was very minute, and conformity to laws apparently trivial was deemed important as testing and developing character. Every commercial establishment, especially if it be large, is like a well-managed ship, under a necessity of being governed by some specific rules; and conformity to them is rightfully expected. Even if the rules relate to *small matters*, their observance is important in this connection; for the benefit of strictness is twofold, affecting both the mind of the employer and your own. Evidently, it gains his confidence for you, and places his mind more at ease in regard to the course of his affairs when he is absent from home. This feeling is to him of great value, and is produced in his bosom as much by a strict conformity to his wishes in *little* things as in the management of great transactions. Once, a merchant of New York, while travelling in the distant West, was heard to say that he was free from all anxiety about the business that he had left behind him, on account of his entire confidence in his head-clerk, who, though at that time quite a youth, let nothing within his province escape his attention. Surely, the mental quiet which such a confidence produces is worth to any man no ordinary price.

Moreover, this habit of strict conformity to an employer's wishes in the smallest matters *reäcts* favorably on one's own character; for surely, he is best qualified to take care of his own interests who has learned to look well after those which another man has committed to him. He who has been careful of his employer's property, is thereby fitted to husband property for himself, and he who gains a reputation for strict fidelity will lay up a good store "against the time to come."

But are there not cases to which these remarks do not apply? Undoubtedly, where the rules themselves are founded in wrong, and are the mere instruments of fraud and chicanery; where they contravene the command of God, which is the Law of laws, conformity would insure the forfeiture of his blessing and of your own mental peace. If the business itself which is proposed to you be a bane to society, "touch it not, handle it not." If it be good in itself, but be conducted by rules which strike at the root of public virtue and fair dealing, yield not up to the moral chains and slavery which they impose, for the iron thereof will enter into thy own soul. The bondage which hampers only the body while it leaves the spirit free and serene, is more tolerable than that which forces a man to act contrary to his convictions of right, robs him of his self-respect, turns conscience into a foe, jeopards his salvation, and arrays against him the workings of an overruling Providence. A man may bear with the frown of his fellow, with the loss of a place, but these other evils are still more terrible, and may be eternal. The pains of the flesh are, on the whole, short-lived; those of "the inner man" are immortal as the soul itself. As saith the Scripture, "The spirit of a man may sustain his infirmity, but a *wounded spirit* who can bear?"

We can easily imagine, however, that some may reply, All this is true; it is very proper that such things should be said and written by moral teachers; but we are the victims of a corrupting system from which the way of extrication is not easy or obvious; we did not originate it, but find ourselves encircled within the ample folds of this mighty net-work, "like the fish of the sea, made to be snared and taken." If there were but few whose demands are at war with our consciences, we could quickly get relief; but now, the alternative before us is, that we do wrong or starve. Change the system, break down prevailing customs, and then we, one by one, can carry out our resolutions.

But is it so? Must you sacrifice integrity for bread? Must you, in fact, cheat or beg? Must you do those things in trade from which the Turk, guided only by his Koran, recoils with indignation? And do you yield to the evil from a feeling of necessity, make that your apology, and thus drug your conscience with opiates, lest you writhe under its sting? If it be so, your case is hard, very hard; and, in some respects, more deplorable than that of those whose bodies were the victims of Algerine captivity. But what is to be done? First, we must say in answer to this question, that if the circumstances of your probation are made so severe by the corrupted principles of trade, the thing to be done is, not to wait for the alteration of the system, but to strengthen in your heart the principle of resistance. Rise superior to the system. Such a moral heroism is not quixotic. Many have put it forth in practice, and have triumphed. We have known young men who have refused to change invoices, or make false entries, or say that an article cost more than it did, or engage in any kind of false dealing, who have seemed to risk every thing, but, in fact, have at last gained every thing. The trial may be severe, but the triumph will be the greater. Therefore, "to yourself be true;" "have faith in God;" for mighty is the truth and will prevail.

Then again, observe, in regard to the great system of trade, if the majority, or a large proportion of the *youth* of this country were imbued with such a morally heroic spirit as would strengthen them to take a just position in favor of honorable dealing, trade would be relieved from the stigma cast upon it, because the system would thus become conformed to the law of rectitude. If the principles of truth and justice were impressed effectually on one generation by the teachings of the family, the public-school, the Sabbath-school, the sanctuary, and by individual examples, our national character would be brightened, the snares of business would be removed, the realm of trade would not be so thickly set with traps for consciences, and succeeding generations would start forth on their career with greater advantages.

Let not the young clerk or apprentice, therefore, succumb to wrong, saying in a desponding tone, "I have no influence; I must submit and bide my time." Carry out into action your knowledge of the RIGHT, and you may have more power than you suppose. The Almighty Ruler of the universe will prove himself the patron of virtue, and will be your helper. Take his Word for your guide. Let the principles laid down in the book of Proverbs form your rules. Then, if constrained to differ from your seniors, let it be seen by your prompt attention to every duty, and by the courteousness of your manners, and by your generous efforts to please them, that you are governed by no mere whim, by no element of fanaticism, but by the dictates of reason, of conscience, and of Christianity. Surely, in this way, you will not only win respect, but will find all the ministries of Heaven, and all the workings of Providence, to be on your side. As the voice of a child has been the occasion of a reform in a family, when all higher teachings had been in vain, so a young man who maintains his integrity amidst corrupting scenes of business, may put forth an influence more far-reaching than his voice, penetrating as light, and purifying as a hidden fire.

III. A third observation which suggests itself in this connection, relates to the *duty of self-improvement.* Be firmly resolved to cultivate your intellectual and moral nature. In carrying out such a resolution, three things demand special care. (1.) The first is a good economy of those hours which may be at your own disposal. Probably there is many a young man to whom the thought will occur, when this subject is mentioned, that he has so little time at his command, any purposes which he may form respecting it would not amount to much. Yet certain it is that he who knows not the value of a little time, so as to make it tell on some result, would squander much if he had it in his power to do so. TIME IS MONEY, says Franklin; and surely, he who throws away cents will waste dollars; so, he who is careless of minutes will waste hours. "Young gentlemen," once said Prof. Anthon to a class of Freshmen, "I doubt not you will all make good scholars, if no one of you will imagine that *ten minutes* is too small a fragment of time to use profitably in study." A great deal may sometimes be done in ten minutes. Attention to a remark like that has made the fortune of many a student. For want of sober calculation on this point, many useful things which might be done, are never attempted. To illustrate this, observe the following conversation, which, in substance, took place between a young clerk and his old teacher in the Sunday-school.

Teacher.—Some time ago, you mentioned to me that you had no doubt that the acquisition of the French and Spanish languages would be of great service to you in the course of your business. Have you yet undertaken to learn either of them?

Clerk.—No, Sir; I have been discouraged by the want of time.

T.—Why, have you not a single hour out of the twenty-four at your command for any study?

C.—Yes, I could get that, but it would be a slow work to acquire a language in that way.

T.—Suppose that you had nothing to do for the next two months—would you make a beginning?

C.—Immediately.

T.—Probably, in your active business life, there never will come a year when you will have more than two months' vacation. And if you had, it would not be for the health of your body or mind to devote more than five unbroken hours every day to close study. If, however, you should do that, you might make great proficiency in the acquisition of a language within the period we have mentioned.

C.—True; I have no doubt of it.

T.—Shall I tell you how to gain that time this year?

C.—I should be glad to know.

T.—Well—begin and persevere in using your one hour a day. Five hours' study per day for two months (leaving out Sundays) would make about 265 hours. But one hour's study per day for a year (leaving out Sundays) would be 313 hours, so that you have at command more than two months of study the present year. And one hour a day for a year, well employed, would enable you to accomplish more in the study of a modern language for purposes of business, than the whole of that time given to you in a mass.

We believe this view of the case to be just. And how obvious is it that this remark applies not only to the study of a language, but to the study of political economy, or of history, or of the Bible, or of any other subject; and how applicable are the words of the poet, who says,

> "The shortest space which we so lightly prize
> When it is coming, and before our eyes—
> Let it but slide into the eternal main,
> No realms, no worlds can purchase it again."

(2.) Connected with the right use of time is the right use of MONEY. "He who is faithful in the least, is faithful also in that which is much;" and he who has learned how to spend well his pocket-money while young, is preparing to appropriate large sums prudently in maturer years. The habit of spending immense sums uselessly in manhood, comes of spending small sums worse than uselessly in early life.

It was a good suggestion which was once made by a clergyman to a young married couple, when they were about to commence housekeeping, to procure a neat book-case, and to fill it only as they might have opportunity to procure such select works as they needed It stood a long time in its place before it was well stored, but it was an object of interest to both of them to devote what money they could spare in order to supply its empty shelves; and when at last they saw it filled with volumes, most of which they had read together, they would not have parted with them for twice their cost. How much more satisfactory were such mementoes of money spent, than an account-book filled with the memoranda of the same amount dissipated in trifling amusements, like precious seed scattered on arid sands, to perish fruitlessly! The suggestion here referred to is as applicable to a young man who has a room to himself, as to those who are heads of families.

(3.) Connected with the right employment of time and money, as a means of self-improvement, is the faithful use of THE SABBATH. In the conversation which we have cited, between the old teacher and the young clerk, respecting the worth of an hour per day throughout the year, for purposes of study, the Sabbaths were properly left out of the calculation, because these are appropriated by the Author of our being to the care of our spiritual interests. Fifty-two Sabbaths a year is the birthright of every man, of which he may not lawfully be deprived, and which no one may sell for a mess of pottage. Whatever might be the price in such a traffic, it would, at last, seem mean enough, compared with the value sacrificed. If your Sabbaths be habitually misspent, every good pı nciple of your character will be weakened. When I think of a man posting books, all enwrapped in business on this sacred day, whose winged hours, stealing softly by, seem to invite his thoughts to the infinite and the eternal, I imagine that I hear the angel of destiny proclaim, "He is joined to his idols; let him alone." With equal power does this solemn sentence arouse my fears when I observe a young man yielding to the temptation which entices him to take the Sabbath for rides, and sports, and sensual recreations; as if the Divine provisions for his moral good were superfluous; as if indeed he had no soul to save. In this way his spiritual energies are destroyed. Yet true it is that every Sabbath renews, in some form, the temptations described in the early part of our Saviour's history. When the Sabbath-bell calls man to "worship the Lord our God, and him only to serve," then the evil one holds forth the baits of sensual pleasure, saying, "These will I give thee if thou wilt fall down and worship me." But to accept these terms is to make a wretched bargain. These rosy, blooming pleasures soon shed their fragrance. By these "man cannot live." A good plan of spending the Sabbath is of inestimable worth, and this, in every case where it is possible, embraces the engaging a seat in some particular church—a seat which one can call his own—occupying it regularly, and also some hours set apart for religious reading. He who is faithful in this, will have reason to adopt a sentiment of Mr. Wilberforce, recorded in his journal:

"I thank God for the institution of the Sabbath; and may I so use it as to find that by its means my errors are corrected, my desires after good quickened, and my whole soul animated in my Christian course!"

IV. It may not be amiss to add a few words in regard to the *choice of friends*. You will have need of a friend, one or more, on whom you can rely for sympathy and counsel. "But a faithful friend, who can find?" The question implies a difficulty, not an impossibility. An oriental writer has said, "Be in peace with many, nevertheless have but one counsellor of a thousand." Trust not the over-credulous—for his judgment is not good: nor, on the other hand, trust the over-suspicious; for when a man distrusts all others, he is unsound at heart. Put not yourself in the power of a covetous person, especially if he be an old man; for there is no kindness in his bosom. And if he be professedly religious, it is very likely that his theory of religion makes covetousness a virtue under the name of frugality. Beware of him, for he is conscientiously cruel. Beware also of slighting religion itself on his account, for it would be foolish to wrong your own soul because you can prove your neighbor a hypocrite. In every engagement with such a one, however, be exact to the letter, and be not satisfied to leave any point with his saying, "I'll do what is right about it." The supreme love of money is a hellish as well as an earthly passion; it denies the reality of a generous spirit, it mocks at mercy, it confounds all distinction between right and wrong, between justice and oppression. If you would gain true friends yourself, you must aim to be worthy of them; for the wise man well said, "He that hath friends must show himself friendly."

Friendly reader! I would close these remarks by wishing you success in the business of your life. But why should I breathe such a wish? Merely for the enjoyment which success may confer during the brief period of this your fitful, feverish existence? No. That would be too mean an object to fill the heart of a Christian man, too low to awaken a desire so strong as that with which this wish is uttered. It is that, acting in accordance with the principles here suggested, you may nobly fulfil your mission to the world, "serve well your generation," your country, and your race—that in all things pleasing Christ, who, "though he was rich, yet for our sakes became poor, that we through his poverty might become rich," your success on earth may enhance your treasure in heaven. Be sure, first of all, that you dedicate your heart, your faculties, and your property to his service. Then, when He who hath said, "Occupy till I come," shall summon you to the reckoning, you will not dread the meeting, but will hail it with a welcome, and hear that approving sentence, which enfolds within itself all eternal blessings, "Well done, faithful servant: thou hast been faithful over a few things, I will make thee RULER OVER MANY THINGS: enter thou into the joy of thy Lord."

The Use and Abuse of Amusements.

"THEY THAT USE THIS WORLD, AS NOT ABUSING IT."

IN our reasonings touching matters of right and wrong, how often does it happen that whilst our perceptions of general principles are clear, nevertheless, when we come to apply those principles in practice, the judgment falters at the point of action, so that we grope like travellers who are suddenly surrounded by a bewildering mist! The difficulties that perplex us in such cases spring mainly from the varying, doubtful aspects which certain practices assume; now, perhaps, from the ill effects which have followed what seemed to be a good, and now, again, from the seeming benefits and the high examples which sustain and honor what we had deemed a real evil. Something adventitious to the subject has distracted the mind in every effort to decide the moral character of the thing in question. The habit of *social drinking*, for instance, which has made so many millions of wretched victims, has recommended itself to young and ingenuous minds more by incidental associations than by its own intrinsic charms; more by the fashion which upheld it and the names which dignified it than by its own power of temptation. These adventitious circumstances have thrown around it an alluring guise, by means of which it has fatally enamored many who would have spurned it from them had they tried it at first by any fixed principle of morals; but who, at last, have yielded to its sway as completely as did that old Roman who declared that he would sooner believe drunkenness to be right than that Cato could be guilty of doing wrong. Thus has it happened sometimes in regard to a number of fashionable amusements. Many a man of social spirit, many a youthful Christian has carelessly complied with the invitation of some friend, or party, to visit a chosen resort, and to wile away an evening hour in some favorite amusement. While scarcely conscious of it, he has breathed a tainted atmosphere; his taste has become vitiated, and his moral feelings somewhat benumbed. Then, if he have any principles, he is unable to apply them with decision; and if he have none, he is wont to imagine that his own good sense will teach him "how far to go." Fatal mistake! He is really out on life's deceitful sea, like a bark without a helm of sufficient power to command her course over the stormy surge or drifting current. A young man moving amidst scenes of excitement, where Fashion holds her court and utters her decrees to pliant throngs, without any principles to guide him in the choice of amusements, determining every question concerning them merely by taste and impulse, can no more distinguish the good from the evil than an infant can distinguish between medicine and poison. The very slave, the devotee of amusement, he must become, for there is no law of the universe to interfere with that result. The passion for amusement "grows by what it feeds on," and, ever loth to keep its place as a servant to the reason, aspires to guide and reign. Always craving and insatiate, it follows temptation blindly, and then, amidst many bitter disappointments, verifies a poetic description of its nature:

> That love of pleasure, endless thirst,
> Which e'en by quenching is awaked,
> And which becomes or blest or curst
> As is the fount whereat 'tis slaked.

According to their use or their abuse, amusements may become the means of enlivening or of paralyzing the moral powers, of strengthening or of weakening the intellect, of quickening the whole soul into a healthful and joyous activity, or of bringing over it a deadly torpor to disqualify it for all its high and serious duties. Better would it be to have none than those which generally prove to be mere baits to ruin—nets spread around the paths of society to decoy and entrap the unsuspecting. But as the abuse of them furnishes no solid argument against their proper use, I will now proceed to consider,

I. The Necessity and Design of Amusements.
II. Some Principles which may guide us in the choice of them.

The first topic involves the inquiry whether amusement is *needed* to supply the real wants of our nature. In regard to this point, it appears to us that the history of our race, the human constitution, the tendencies of childhood, the means of enjoyment provided by our Creator, all indicate that amusement is not only allowable, but necessary for us. The necessity arises from the unalterable condition in which man finds himself. In all the relations of life he has important duties to perform, and faculties adapted to their performance. Connected with all these relations and duties, there is somewhat of labor, responsibility and care, which tend to exhaust our energies; and which, if permitted to press beyond a certain limit, impair the power of action. The most industrious often suspend their labors with a sigh; and if they do not learn the proper bound whereat to pause, a derangement or destruction of the faculties must ensue. One of the most devoted workers in the cause of humanity, acknowledged in his last sickness that he had erred by this inattention to the laws of his nature, and that he was dying on account of having had too much to do. Sir Humphry Davy, by the incessant tension of his mind in his chemical pursuits, induced a disease which brought him to the verge of the grave in the midst of his usefulness. The old proverb, "It is better to wear out than to rust out," is undoubtedly true; but it is wrong to become deaf to that voice of nature which demands a constant alternation of action and repose. In such a case, where God's law is plain, a persevering and wilful transgression of it would be akin to the crime of suicide. Every one can see that, as it would be sinful to stimulate our faculties to an unnatural intensity of action by any poisonous drug which, in the end, must weaken them, so, voluntarily to overwork them when they cry out for rest or refreshment, is a thing in its nature wrongful. Justice and mercy both forbid us to overwork a beast; and when men, mad with the love of money, have denied themselves all the means of domestic and social enjoyment until they have become the victims of incessant toil, they have been condemned by the universal suffrage of the world for having neglected the duties which they owed to themselves, to their country, and their God.

We need not wonder, therefore, that in the history of the earliest ages, and of every people, the common amusements form an important feature. In patriarchal times, the cares of pastoral life in the East were lightened by festivals, by rural sports and music; and all joyous occasions were signalized by mirth and songs, accompanied by the tabret and the harp. When the Jewish people assumed a more compact form, with a code of laws and a ritual, this want of our nature was provided for; their holidays were numerous, and their religious service was not only distinguished by the awful and the grand, but by its tendency to inspire vivacity and cheerfulness.

Indeed, our views of the character of a people must be very deficient, unless we have a knowledge of their prevailing amusements. We are not to judge of them by these only, but these are never to be overlooked in relation to the classes who favor or oppose them. What can give us a clearer idea of the fatal sway with which the love of pleasure ruled the Athenians, than to consider that it was by means of the THEATRE that the enemies of Socrates procured his death; that notwithstanding all the reverence which the people felt towards the philosopher, and all their gratitude for the renown which he had brought to his country, their sentiments were quickly changed under the spell of a comedy filled with satire from the pen of Aristophanes, by whom they were thus impelled to pass that act of condemnation which inflicted a deep wound on the republic, filled their own bosoms with shame, and has drawn from the men of every succeeding generation the tears of sympathy and sadness? What can exhibit more vividly the heroic sternness which characterized the Roman people than their refusal to allow their priests, or statesmen, or honorable youth, to associate with those whose profession was play-acting? And what more clearly shows the need of the softening influence of pure religion to prevent that rigid heroism from degenerating into absolute cruelty, than to look at the amusements of their vast and splendid amphitheatres? There, what a scene of grandeur and of terror greets your eyes, when thirty thousand people are assembled and ranged on seats which rise one above another in beautiful gradation around a circle or an ellipse, waiting for the promised entertainment! Hark to those shouts of the multitude! Behold the naked gladiators entering from opposite points, proud in their bearing, whilst they attract the gaze of so much rank and wealth, and youth and beauty; then, the brandishing of their dazzling blades, the fierce onset—the strength and skill displayed by each; the thrust, the foil, the rapid pass, the parrying stroke, the effective blow—the alternation of hope and doubt, of triumph and despair—the loss of blood, the faintness, the reeling, the last agony, the fall of the unfortunate combatant, and the quick appeal which flashed from the conqueror's eye, as, with his foot upon his victim's neck, he looked towards the mighty crowd, in order to learn from the turning of their thumbs, whether he should kill or spare a prostrate foe, whom he would fain butcher, "to make a Roman holiday."

Well did the old Athenian exclaim, when it was proposed to introduce these combats into his beloved city, "First break down the altar of Mercy which our ancestors have erected."

Nothing is more evident than that, while amusement is to be recognized as a want of our condition, it is in itself very liable to abuse, because it addresses the weaker parts of our nature; approaches us with the aspect of a tempter; if indulged a little too far, tends by its fascinations to lessen our zest for serious business, proposes itself as the *chief* business, seeks to rule where it ought to serve, unnerves where it ought to strengthen, and destroys where it ought to build up a noble and manly character. To prevent such issues, it must be kept true to its legitimate design, which is best expressed by a word, often used as synonymous. That word is RECREATION. To re-create the energies of the nervous system, to soothe and exhilarate the mind, to impart to it a healthful tone and to render it more apt for all its duties, is the proper purpose of amusement. It is needed therefore, more or less, by all; because, as we have already said, the mind is like the bow—"o'er-bend it, and it breaks." Yet, this strong hold which it has upon our nature, makes it an element of power which may be wielded for great good or evil. Hence, it has been seized with avidity, and made to play an important part in the schemes of those who would prevent men from rising to the dignity of self-government—of those who, in order to make others their tools, would first weaken them by vice—of despots, who, to establish their authority securely, have studied all the arts of keeping the people quiet. On the Continent of Europe it is the aim of the royal governments to have "the masses" all-engrossed with amusement. They use the money of the nation to corrupt it, and tempt the active spirits of the multitude to desecrate the Sabbath, and to waste their time in spectacles and sports. When the Emperor Napoleon observed one day that the Parisians were rather restless, pointing to a splendid edifice within sight from his window, he gave the order, "Go—gild the dome of yonder hospital." Paris, he saw, must have something to look at and talk about. So, now, the government of France is as careful to appropriate money to support the theatre, as to support a standing army. In Italy, the traveller, having arrived at Rome, notices that *church-ceremonies* are set down in his guide-book among the amusements of the place, and the Papal court is liberal in providing shows of other kinds. In Austria, the Emperor is called the father of the people—his government is styled paternal; accordingly, throughout the empire none of his children, great or small, can pass the boundary without permission; and over them all he seems to watch with deep solicitude lest they should be injured by going from home, or by mingling too freely with strangers. Foreigners are tracked by spies as keen in their pursuit as hounds scenting their game; and foreign literature, scanned at first with suspicious look, is often condemned with Vandal rudeness. A strange book in a traveller's package is handled as if it might contain the plague. New light and knowledge are fenced out of the realm, and to the officers of state, foreign newspapers are objects of dread and horror. To balance these restrictions, the people are supplied richly with amusements; Vienna is made one of the most lively of capitals, and a public, thus engrossed, have a universal air of ease and gayety. Some American tourists have seemed to envy them all this, and to wish that here, at home, we had more of their constant hilarity. But why should the lack of this be a subject of complaint? If this Austrian happiness be a blessing, it can be procured as cheaply by us as by any other people. Doubtless, in this land there are statesmen, naturally wise and liberal, who would furnish us all with amusements at their own expense, if we would allow them to tax us, support a standing army, and manage our affairs as they please. This freedom from care is a privilege which will always be in the market, when the people are willing to pay their LIBERTY as its price. And this they will surely be willing to do, if amusements should here become a popular idol; if a passion for it should reign in our youth without control, should grow with their growth, strengthen with their strength, and absorb the energy of manhood. Then, Americans would have no moral force whatsoever to resist the wiles and the demands of those political desperadoes of whom every age brings forth its share. What was it that paralyzed the nerve and took away the heart of Athens, once able to set all Asia at defiance? It was the idolatry of amusement, nourished by Pericles, an ambitious corrupter of her own sons, who, notwithstanding all the splendors of his administration, and all the memorials of art that he left, did more to lay her glory in the dust than all her foes of Persia or Macedon. And if now, in the progress of European manners and influence amongst us, the supreme love of amusement shall enervate the character of our American youth, they will be utterly unfitted for the strife of mind, the toils and cares necessary to sustain a republican government, and will sink down passively under the sway of those who by the energy of their nature will verify the pretension that they were "born to command."

If, then, recreation be a want of man, if it be necessarily liable to abuse, even to degenerate into low and dissipating amusements, let us see if we can guard against the evil, and yet secure the good. In order to do this, we will set forth,

II. Principles which are tests of the character of Amusements.

Every amusement which addresses itself to unhallowed passions must be disallowed by the Christian law. Such are all those which involve *cruelty* in their pursuit, as did the lion-fights of Rome, as do the bull-fights of Spain and South America, the fights of game-birds in England and in this country, as well as those pugilistic combats which have of late presented such spectacles of sin and shame in some portions of our land.

Proscribed, too, by this law, are all forms of GAMING in which one's success must be at another's expense, and which are ever tending to awaken suspicion, jealousy, envy, fixed malice, wrath, strife, despair. We know that there is much in a name, and certainly, the vocabulary of this world was never more accurate than in designating as *hells* those places where the spirit of gambling reigns. All fiend-like passions riot there; and to see those passions in full play, and all the horrible issues to which they lead, would shock the soul of that young man who may be now taking the first steps in that career which reaches unto such a fearful termination. Yes, you who say, "I'll play a little, but within proper bounds—will carefully control myself, and never hazard all upon a single throw," remember that those men whose aspect is so revolting, and whose hearts are so desperate, thus began, impelled by that love of excitement which now tempts you to touch and handle—which grows by each indulgence, and, though at present a gentle zephyr which you can guide, must soon become a furious blast to drive you onward,

> Like a ship dashed by fierce encountering tides,
> And of her pilot spoiled.

The biography of gamblers will furnish manifold proof of my assertion on this point. One who had wasted much of his life in this way in New York, said, in answer to the question, What was the largest sum which you ever won at a sitting?—"Why, when I was a young fellow, I won one night thirty thousand dollars at a brag. I played all night, and lost it all back except eight hundred dollars; and I would have lost that, but that it was Sunday morning, and hearing the bells ring for church, I recollected that I had promised my wife to go and hear the Bishop preach. So, I washed my face and hands, smoothed my hair, and with downcast looks and pious features, joined in the Litany and chanted the Psalms."

But did you never forswear gaming?

"Oh, frequently, but always broke my oath. One night I lost three thousand dollars—all I had in the world. I walked home with a friend, in a melancholy mood; it was past two o'clock, and I invited him to drink a glass of brandy and water. I swore all the bitter oaths I could remember, that I never would handle cards again. While I was thus swearing, feeling in my pockets for a little loose tobacco, I found a bank note of a hundred dollars. All my gaming propensities revived in an instant! Let's go back, said I, and try our luck once more; with this hundred I may win five thousand. I went back, and lost the note in five minutes; and here I am, not worth a penny."

What chain could be more galling than this, which a man who thought himself free had forged for his own soul?

Now, he who considers from what small beginnings gigantic vices grow, and the power which is exercised over the young mind by these two simple elements, —the desire of society and the love of excitement,—need not wonder that men of observation, who have seen much of the world and its ways, should believe that the practice of *card-playing*, even for trifling sums, which is indulged by many a youthful circle, nourishes a germ of evil; nor that such a clear-sighted reasoner as the celebrated John Locke should congratulate himself that, though he had kept house nearly forty years, had been surrounded with a large family, and had entertained much company, yet he never had cards, dice, or any implement of gaming, under his roof. "The hours," says he, "that young men spend in this way are murdered—precious hours which ought to be spent in reading or writing, or rest preparatory to the dawn." How could a man of sense like him look with any other emotion than that of pity on a company of human beings doomed to pass an evening together, yet lacking so much the power of entertaining conversation, as to be obliged to spend their time in gazing at bits of paper marked with parti-colored spots, caring for nothing but to "kill time;" and yet, perhaps, fostering a fatal passion which some day may break out like a fire from under the smouldering ashes, and consume the bosom that it warmed?

Those amusements, moreover, which arouse a passion for personal display, (always involving, as it does, those of vanity and envy,) amusements which absorb much time and thought in preparation, and tend to exhaust one's nature in their process; which cherish a spirit of competition, not for intellectual excellence, but for superior elegance in dress and movement, have been generally seen to be adverse to this Christian law. We speak of those of which the words of the old poet, Shirley, are descriptive:

> Another game you have which consumes more
> Your fame than purse; your revels in the night,
> Your meetings called the BALL; to which repair,
> As to the court of pleasure, all your gallants
> And ladies.

It has been the fashion in some quarters to regard a disapprobation of the ball as an amusement to be one of the peculiarities of Puritanism. But this is far from being true. The fact that the Puritans were adverse to it may have its proper weight, but it is not a sufficient argument against it. Touching the real merits of the ball as a recreation, let me cite the words of one who cannot be suspected of any thing very rigid in his notions—of one who was neither a friend to the Puritans, nor to Christianity itself. "Although," says Gibbon in his great work on the Decline and Fall of the Roman Empire, "the progress of civilization has undoubtedly contributed to assuage the fiercer passions of human nature, it seems to have been less favorable to the virtue of chastity, whose most dangerous enemy is the softness of the mind. The refinements of life corrupt while they polish the intercourse of the sexes. The gross appetite of love becomes most dangerous when it is elevated, or rather, indeed, disguised by sentimental passion. The elegance of dress, of motion, and of manners, gives a lustre to beauty, and inflames the senses through the imagination. Luxurious entertainments, midnight dances, and licentious plays, present at once temptation and opportunity to female frailty."* These sentences, from the pen of one who loved to plunge in all the pleasures of a European capital, explain the philosophy of this amusement, show the reason why it is considerd dangerous, and just where the danger lurks. If this be true, undoubtedly the atmosphere of a ball-room must be uncongenial with the spirit of a religion which cultivates only pure affections, quickens the aspirations of the soul after goodness, and educates it on earth for the society of heaven.

The liability of the art of dancing to various abuses, its connection with the evils above mentioned, have furnished to many Christian parents strong reasons for withholding the knowledge of it from their children. Hence, too, there have often sprung up in the bosom of a well-ordered family, discussions between the older and the younger members of it as to the merits of the case. Sometimes I have found young Christians, between the ages of eighteen and twenty-five years, whose sphere of social intercourse was quite extensive, oppressed with difficulty in regard to danc-

---

* Decline and Fall of the Roman Empire, chap. ix.

ing, on account of their inability to vindicate or explain the opposition to it under all circumstances, which they have found to exist on the part of their parents, their friends, and their church. The difficulty which they have felt may be stated somewhat thus: It must be admitted, that there can be nothing abstractly wrong in dancing, because it was once sanctioned of Heaven, and practised in religious service. God could never approve what was wrong in its nature, or necessarily bad. But if religiously approved and practised once, why should it not be so now? On what grounds should pious persons be expected to oppose that which has in its favor the examples of the best of men, and of all the Jewish people? Can that be wrong in social life, which was once a part of divine service among the tribes of Israel?*

These are fair questions, and should be fairly treated. The nature of that opposition to dancing as an amusement, which multitudes of Christians, distinguished by refinement, wealth, and taste, have cherished, may be more fully comprehended, if we will look at the subject *historically*. Let it be observed, then, that the social dancing of modern Europe, which has been transferred to America, is neither Jewish, religious, nor simply *calisthenic*, as to its origin, but is a daughter of the Roman dance, which was ever associated with licentiousness. The Greeks had cultivated the art of dancing with an extravagant passion, and were the first to introduce hired dancers into the theatre; the Romans

* Ex. xv 20. 1 Sam. xviii. 6.

followed their example, and thus fixed a stigma on what had before been deemed a sacred rite or an innocent recreation. Before Christianity was known in Rome, the respectable portion of society frowned on these dances. Cicero objected against a Senator, that he had fallen from the dignity of his station by being seen to dance;* and the satires of Juvenal prove that in a succeeding age, these amusements had shamefully depraved the public manners. At different times, the Roman Government, under Tiberius and Domitian, passed severe decrees against them. Of course, we need not wonder that the writings of the early Christians abound with sharp invectives against a public amusement on which the Pagan moralists themselves had stamped the impress of dishonor.

During the reign of Gothic and Vandal barbarism over the Roman Empire in the middle ages, very little attention was paid to any of the refinements of life. But when the modern art of dancing arose in Europe, it was surrounded with all those associations which would cause religious persons to revolt from it. At the festivals of the Italian nobles it was first revived, and then it appeared in France. The opera in Paris was originally designed for the representation of lyric poems; but as soon as its popularity began to decline, female dancers were introduced to give a novel zest to the entertainment; an immodest style of dress was allowed for the same purpose, and thus, as early as the age of

---

Cicero says, "Nemo fere saltat solivius, nisi insanit."—Scarcely any unintoxicated man dances, unless, indeed, he is insane.

Louis XIV., the Parisians hailed with acclamation the same gross exhibitions which had been condemned by the better classes of society in pagan Rome. Invested with such associations, modern dancing drew the attention of our religious ancestors in England; it wore no aspect of utility, sacredness, or beauty; and who can wonder that they repelled it from their entertainments, their social circles, and their homes? Although, abstractly considered, they might have seen in it nothing wrong, yet in view of all the circumstances of their times, they were forced to regard the custom as a sort of livery in which the "god of this world" had chosen to array his own votaries. And as now we often find that persons of taste reject the articles of dress and ornament which once were beautiful in their sight, but have afterwards come to appear mean, because adopted by the low and the abandoned; so, the Christians of whom we speak, influenced merely by *moral taste*, rejected an amusement which had once seemed innocent and beautiful, because it had everywhere become one of the insignia of worldliness—a badge of recognition worn by those who pursue no end but pleasure, and worship no God but Fashion.

That dancing, however, is a natural mode of expressing various lively and virtuous emotions, there can be no doubt. When animated with any joyous feeling, our very nature prompts us to move, even "the lame to leap as an hart;" and when a number of persons are excited by the same cause, as music, poetry, or oratory, they naturally tend to move together. The Welsh people, who are, as all know, very excitable, have been seen to dance under the influence of a sermon from one of their stirring preachers. This unrestrained mode of manifesting feeling, nevertheless, belongs rather to a state of barbarism than of refinement. It is the tendency of civilization to repress all bold and violent methods of expressing emotion. When Christianity arose in the world, dancing had already been abused to purposes of evil, and it was not accordant with the nature of our religion to sanction it as an act of worship. Although the word *choir* in Christian countries originally meant a dancing company, and dancing in religious service was practised among the Papists, yet this is to be classed among the corruptions of Christianity. The Shakers of our own time are the only people who maintain it, and their style of execution, though in some sense impressive, is not remarkably captivating. But whether dancing, viewed simply as a *social recreation*, shall ever be disabused of all its evil connections, and treated with favor throughout the religious community, as it was in the days of the Patriarchs, of Moses, and of David, remains to be seen. It is not in the nature of things impossible. If the state of society should become increasingly pure, such an event would be more and more probable; for then there would be less of fear that what is good in itself would be made a bait to evil. In the combined rhythm of chaste music and motion to express joyfulness, there is nothing incompatible with our ideas of the purity of Eden or of heaven. And if sin were banished from the world, every faculty, and passion, and social tendency of man would be consecrated; truly Christian minds would give the tone to society; the laws of fashion would be coincident with the laws of God, and all art, science, and literature, wealth, music and song, would be friendly to religion, and enjoyed without the dread of perversion. But the more corrupt we find the social condition in which we live, the more need is there of caution for a Christian man in the use of things which in themselves are harmless; just as it was in the case mentioned in his letter to the Corinthians by the Apostle Paul, who declared, that though it were quite an innocent thing in itself to go to a social feast and partake of meat in a temple of idolatry, yet sooner would he abjure meat for ever, than ensnare another to pay an act of worship at an idol's shrine.

Viewed simply as a *calisthenic* exercise in the education of children, the practice of the elementary parts of dancing has often proved to be beneficial. Regarding it in this light it is that Dr. Watts observes, in his treatise on the education of children: "I confess I see no evil in it. It is a healthful exercise, and it gives young persons a decent manner of appearance in company; it may be profitable to some good purposes if it be well guarded against all the abuses and temptations that may attend it." It is properly a child's amusement, and has its place in a good system of healthful, physical training. The philosopher Locke, in his work on education, makes a remark similar to that which I have quoted from the sacred poet. Mrs. Sigourney, too, in her letters to young ladies, aptly cites the observation of Addison, that the principal use of a lady's being taught dancing is, that she may "know how to sit still gracefully;" and then proceeds to say, "As a mode of exercise in the *domestic* circle, it is healthful, and favorable to a cheerful flow of spirits. I was once accustomed to witness it in a happy family, where the children, at the close of the reading and lessons which diversified the long winter evenings, rose to the music of the piano, while the parents, and even grandparents, mingling with the blooming circle, gave dignity to the innocent hilarity in which they participated. There was nothing in this to war with the spirit of the prayers which were soon to follow, or to indispose to that hymn of praise which hallowed their nightly rest." A scene like this might, indeed, seem tame to one who had become fascinated with the gayeties of the ball-room, where the eye is dazzled, the blood fevered, the night far spent, and the thoughts engrossed with vanity; but to a mind in health, it will have a charm superior to all that, because more congenial with purity of heart and the substantial joys of home.

Let us now advance to the establishment of another principle which may be fairly considered as a criterion of amusements. My second position is this: EVERY AMUSEMENT WHICH NATURALLY TENDS TO UNFIT ONE FOR THE ENJOYMENT OF THE HIGHEST HAPPINESS OF WHICH HE IS CAPABLE, IS IN ITSELF MORALLY WRONG. Is not this self-evident? Of course, it is clear that any thing which is at war with man's attaining the highest end of his being must be an evil. Man is constituted with a sensitive, a social, an intellectual, and a moral nature. In each of these are sources of happiness. That which arises from a sensitive nature, we have in common with the brutes. But in the faculties of this lower nature they excel us. Who of our race hath the eye of the eagle, the scent of the hound, the speed of the horse, or the strength of the lion? Man's glory is not in his senses, nor does his real happiness lie within their scope. His highest faculties are those by which he is distinguished from the brute creation, those which enable him to discern between right and wrong—to approve the one and hate the other; those by which he can see God in all his works, adore and serve that Being whose love appears in all the round of his eternal laws, and whose creative wisdom shines alike in the structure of the glow-worm and of the star. To man, then, what consuming curses, what masked assassins are those pleasures which disqualify him for enjoying the bliss which springs from the exercise of the noblest attributes of his nature! Such a thing is that habit of *social drinking* through which every thing rational, dignified, and immortal in us, is made an oblation at the shrine of amusement. For it deserves to be remembered that those generous souls, those "shining marks" at which the monster Intemperance aims his shafts, are not those who drink at first to gratify an appetite, but to gratify a social instinct. When the power of mutual entertainment flags, the stimulating cup is seized to send the blood more swiftly through the veins, and to quicken the spirit of hilarity. A group of young men met at some chosen resort to pass an evening, simply for the want of some mental incitement, often find that their time moves heavily; then wine is made to supply the place of wit and of all intellectual culture. Each repetition makes them more dependent on the inebriating draught for all their "flow of soul," and thus each one chains down to sense his immortal spirit, blights its sweetest hopes, and crushes in the germ its opening capacities.

I have now laid down two principles as tests of amusements, as aids to our choice of them. If by one or both of these principles you try the THEATRE, it must be condemned as being in its nature and tendencies the foe of social morality and the public welfare. In discussing this subject, however, it is a very common thing for writers and speakers to confound all distinction between the drama and the theatre. By the word drama, we mean a poem accommodated to action; a production in which the action is not narrated, but made to pass before you by the persons appearing in their own characters and speaking for themselves. Every dialogue is a drama, and in many cases furnishes the best mode of circulating truth. The Book of Job, the oldest specimen of sacred literature in the world, is a drama. The most pious men have written dramas to illustrate character. The old New England Primer contains a drama—a dialogue between Christ, a youth, and the Devil: no parent would object to his children's reading it; but whether it would be well to fit up a stage and employ persons to act out the characters, is altogether a distinct question from that of the utility of such writings. Evidently, then, to argue, as many do, from the dignity of the drama to the support of a stage and of professional players, is to argue very inconclusively. The two should never be confounded.

Many dramatic writers and readers have opposed the theatre as a social institution, because they have seen it to be in every age allied with wrong, a tempter of youth, and a fountain of corrupting influence.

Yet it has been asked, What harm can there be in the abstract, for a company of persons to meet together, and act out certain historical or imaginary characters? Suffice it to say, in answer to such a question, that whatever the playing may be in the abstract, it always comes to you in the *concrete*, enwrapping many evils. It might be asked with equal reason, What harm can there be in the abstract in one man's writing another's name on a piece of paper? The reply would be, None. But if you do it under a draft for money, the act would be called forgery, and you would be liable to imprisonment if detected. Experience points out evils in practice which do not appear in theory. Hence, even Rousseau, who had no scruples about attending a theatre at Paris, exclaimed against contaminating the society of Geneva by erecting one in that beautiful city.

The experience of ages has shown that a high-minded and moral stage cannot be supported. Just in proportion as mental culture increases, and men become able to enjoy the reading of a drama in their own parlors, the rage for stage exhibitions will be diminished. Some persons who have listened to the lectures of an able critic on Shakspeare, have found that afterwards the magic spell of the stage had for them been broken. They found themselves able to read a drama, either alone or in company, with a delight which they had not known before. Then, no ordinary acting could realize their ideal standards of heroic excellence. Such a fact would naturally work a great change in their mental tastes. Thus, through the united influences of an enlightening civilization and the Christian religion, the theatre has been left to depend for patronage mainly on those who, instead of seeking simple *recreation*, make amusement the chief pursuit; and invariably, in such cases, the passion for amusement destroys a nice sense of moral distinctions, the rage for excitement becomes insanity; and there is a gradual progress from decency to vulgarity, from vulgarity to obscenity, from that to utter lawlessness; so that at last a fashionable audience can gaze without a blush on dancing as licentious as any which was ever seen at a heathen festival, and greet with high applause the woman who, abaning the modesty of her sex, appears in man's attire, walks the broad stage with heavy tramp, and roars with stentorian voice to personify the fiercest of England's warrior-kings. Resting on such a class for support, the theatre will cater for their gross appetites, and so, by a law of nature, must gravitate toward the depths of corruption.

Certainly it is not wonderful that when play-acting becomes a profession, to the members and supporters of it amusement becomes an ultimate object of pursuit. They live for it as an end; and it is impossible that this should be done by any class of human beings without a vitiation of their taste. They become unfit to judge of what is pure or impure. The experience of all times proves the truth of this. Some of the very statements which I have made from observation, would appear, from the poetry of Horace, to have been applicable to the Roman stage. Stage authors and actors, he avers, will descend to the corrupt taste of the people. He describes them as "buffoons with hungry jests," and touching the patrons of the theatre, he exclaims,

> Farewell the stage, for humbly I disclaim
> Such fond pursuits of pleasure or of fame,
> If I must sink in shame or swell with pride,
> As the gay palm is granted or denied:
> And sure the hard, though resolutely bold,
> *Must quit the stage*, or tremble to behold
> The senseless rabble of the clamorous pit,
> Though void of honor, virtue, soul or wit,
> When his most interesting scenes appear,
> Call for a prize-fight, or a baited bear!
> Alas! what fools do now in judgment sit
> In stolid deafness on the works of wit!
> For where's the voice so strong as to confound
> The shouts with which our theatres resound?
> Loud as when surges lash the Tuscan shore,
> Or mountain forests with a tempest roar,
> So loud the people's cries, when they behold
> The foreign arts of luxury and gold;
> And if an actor is but richly drest,
> Their joy is in repeated claps expressed.
> But has he spoken? No. Whence then arose
> That loud applause? His robe with purple glows.

Now, it is a just remark of Sir James Mackintosh, that every poem, every picture, every statue, every work of art, is an experiment on human nature. In the institution of the theatre, we have a long-tried experiment; and what is the result? Is it the improvement of manners, the elevation of taste in the community? Where is the moral difference between that which Horace censured in Rome ten years before the Christian era, and that which has been supported for the last quarter of a century in New York or Boston, or any other capital? That the theatre in its actual operation has aimed to give a certain sort of elevation to the human sentiments, there can be no doubt; bu then, from first to last, it has tended, by the aid of pros tituted beauty and genius, of literature and art, music and song, to send its appeals to the inferior feelings deeply into the soul, to raise them to their highest pitch of excitement, and to kindle the already excessive fires of passion into a more intense and fiercer glow. This is the elevation which it has imparted; the elevation of appetite above reason, of imagination above intellect, of passion above conscience, of the lower part of man's nature above the nobler.

We believe, then, that to be entirely true in relation to the theatre which Bossuet expressed to Lous XIV., who having asked that writer and prelate his opinion on the subject, received for an answer: "Sire, there are for it great examples — there are against it, strong arguments."

Having now considered the necessity and design of amusement, the varied aspects which the subject wears, its peculiar liability to abuse; having laid down several principles to guide us in our choice of them, it is not necessary further that I should take the pains to exhibit in detail a list of recreations which are unobjectionable. Even the best may be perverted in a change of circumstances. Much must be left to the judgment of the individual. Our power of abusing things innocent in themselves, constitutes the most serious part of our probation on the earth, forms the most severe trial of the character. We are too apt to try ourselves only by great occasions and conspicuous deeds; whereas the events of every-day life try us, and prove us, and develop the principles that are within us. We may serve our Creator as effectually by our lighter as by our graver employments if both are kept in their proper relations; and I like well the spirit of the Christian student, who, leaving his study for the playground, told an inquiring friend that he was "going to pitch quoits for the glory of God." Certainly, the acquisition of health for the performance of his work might have been at that moment his highest duty.

So in every thing we should regard the end of our existence. Then all creation will yield us service, and the spirit, serene within, will answer to the rejoicings of nature without. Then, whether a Christian find his recreation on the principle suggested by the old proverb, that "a change of work is as good as a rest," or give scope to his mirthfulness in youthful sports, gymnastic exercises, ball, or battledore, walking, riding, fishing, sailing, or enjoying the fine arts of music, poetry, elocution, painting, sculpture, or indulge his taste for reading and social conversation, or exercise his ingenuity in surrounding his abode with the productions of nature, or scientific mechanism,—amusements which shall heighten the charm of home,—he will feel the happy consciousness that all these are in harmony with the laws of his moral being; that to them he is sacrificing no higher good; that while they increase the vigor of his nerve, the bloom of health, the hilarity of his spirit, they are at the same time occasions of gratitude, wings to devotion, and aids in attaining all the ends of his earthly and his heavenly life.

The Family Library.

"GIVE ATTENDANCE TO READING."—1 Tim. iv. 13.

THERE is scarcely any thing by which the present age is distinguished from times past more than by habits of reading, which have become popular and almost universal. How much these have changed the character and the state of society we cannot clearly understand without some mental effort. Bad as are the effects of those books with which a brilliant mind, animated by the love of money or of fame, now and then floods the market, yet a broad and fair view of things must convince us that, on the whole, the Press is the great elevator of the people. Look back, for instance, a few centuries, and see, throughout the whole of Europe, what a heavy night of ignorance brooded over all classes of minds. Very few could either read or write. Even wealthy nobles were unable to peruse a manuscript, and private life was marred with quarrels about the meaning of bargains and contracts, because so rarely was any thing committed to paper, except treaties, charters, and such grave documents as were written by professional scribes. Place yourself in a court of justice in Germany at any period of the twelfth or thirteenth century, and what a scene greets your eyes! Two men who have brought their cause to the tribunal of the law, are called forth to fight each other with deadly weapons in what is termed a "judicial combat," under the full belief that Providence will interpose to give victory to the right. The decision of the judge on the bench is challenged, and he is obliged to vindicate its justice by a resort to arms. Some are forced to pass the ordeal of exposing their flesh to boiling water, and others to walk with bare feet over burning ploughshares. Strange as these practices may seem to us, they had their origin in a public sentiment for which we can easily account. The natural appetite of man for knowledge was as keen then as it is now; but how was it supplied? With the legends of monks; with wonderful stories of those adventurous saints whose names now shine in the sacred calendar, for whose sake Heaven was constantly working the most stupendous miracles. When men and women, the young and the old, the prince and the peasant, were alike accustomed to receive such fictions for facts, it became, of course, a common belief, that the Almighty might be expected to interfere with the working of general laws in order to protect the innocent; and, being unskilful in the rules of evidence, and impatient of the toil of sifting it, they declared the issue of such trials to have been determined by "the judgment of God." But could such ideas ever prevail in a land where books abound, and where a taste for reading has become popular? By no means. Worthless as are many of the books which in a free country court attention, a people educated to read will always, on the whole, choose those which are far better than the grotesque fables of the cloister, or the queer legends of a superstitious priesthood. Thanks to God that we live in a country where the press is no longer bound, where the children of the rich and poor may learn to read with almost equal ease, where books are scattered abroad like the leaves of the forest, and where, in spite of the power of a corrupting literature, every good man has ample scope to aid in supplying a craving community with the food which is needful.

In such a state of the world, it is very clear that if those of us who are in the prime of life would prepare ourselves for the high destinations to which the signs of the times beckon us, we must make good use of this privilege of READING, which may be fairly ranked among the choicest boons granted of Heaven to this present generation. Towards doing this, how mightily have the aids and stimulants been increased of late! There are those yet alive, in whose youth there were but thirty-seven newspapers in the United States; but now, if we estimate the whole number at fourteen hundred, we shall not be far from the mark. A few years since, the hand-press could cast off but two hundred and fifty sheets per hour; now the steam-press can cast off four thousand in the same time. Once it required five years to prepare a copy of the Bible with a pen; now, Bibles can be printed with a speed adequate to any possible demand. Once a copy of that book would cost a little fortune; now, a laborer can procure five for the amount of a day's work. Within the memory of some printers, a man could cast but five thousand types a day; now, to cast sixty thousand is no extraordinary thing. Once, paper was a costly article made by a tedious process; now, rags gathered from all nations are thrown into a mill, and, with little expense of time and money, they roll out in large and beautiful quires. Once, after waiting some days succeeding the arrival of a packet, a few in the city obtained the news from Europe to peruse quietly by their firesides; now, within two or three hours after the smoke of the steamer is seen off the coast, the news from all lands is selected, printed, cried for sale along the streets—and where is the man too poor to be a purchaser? Once, only grave intelligence travelled abroad; now, the slightest incidents which take place here are carried with lightning speed to the log-cabins of the West, and to the mansions of the eastern world. Science is constantly enlarging her boundaries, creating a new language for herself, so that in every new edition of an English Dictionary, hundreds of new words are inserted as needing to be understood by the student, or as having become familiar among the people.

Now in order that a young man may feel himself at home among men in an age so rife with intellectual activity, he must gain knowledge; in order to gain knowledge, he must read: and surely, it will not do for him to lavish his time on whatever may chance to come to hand, careless whether it be good, bad, or indifferent, thus allowing his mind to become the sport of accident, roving restlessly over the field of literature without a worthy end, without the aim to find and reap substantial fruit. True: much that is good may come in his way, he may pick up much useful information, and all the while may gratify a voracious mental appetite; but it will be seen at last that he utterly fails to command his knowledge, and "digests not into sense his motley meal." He who would bear off from the field of literature enduring wealth, must form a clear conception of the objects to be sought, and must lay out for himself a *course* of reading which will lead him to his chosen ends. If it be his chief desire to gain that general knowledge which will best fit him, as a man and a citizen, for the duties, the enjoyments, and the honors of private and of public life, which will expand all his faculties, and develop his mental character in just and fair proportions, he needs to take in at a glance the various departments of learning, to see the land which he would traverse *mapped* out before him, and to choose those paths which will enable him to give to each province and division the share of attention which it deserves. A little thought bestowed on this subject at the outset, would save to many a vast amount of time, and by leading them to concentrate their powers on works of real utility, would impart a fresh zest to their reading, and make the knowledge which it yields more available.

In offering these few hints to young men, it may be well to state the case in view of which this course of reading was struck out. An esteemed friend, in easy circumstances, but considerably engaged in business, was about to be married soon after he had reached the age of twenty-one. Happening to be with him one day, whilst he was engaged in selecting furniture for the house into which he was expecting shortly to introduce his bride, I urged him to purchase a beautiful book-case which then stood near us. "Why," said he, "I have but few books, and those are so ill-selected, that I should be ashamed to place more than half a dozen of them where they would seem to court inspection." Very well, I replied; you have given me the strongest reason for entreating you to put this case among your choicer articles of furniture; it is just large enough to hold a respectable family library, and with such tastes as you possess, I know that you would be led in due time to have it filled with valuable books, bought not for show but for use. Your brother, who is now ten years of age, is to be one of your household, and his character for life may be formed in a high degree by the books which shall daily greet his eyes from within those glass doors. Buy it, but do not fill it hastily. Fix on a plan of reading; see what books your wants require, and procure such as will be of lasting worth. A good family library is the choicest treasure, light, and ornament of home; it throws out gleams of sunshine in stormy days and nights, by its subtle magnetic power "puts us in communication" with the best minds of all ages, cheers our hours of solitude, and daily imparts new life to the pleasures of conversation. "You are right," said he, "entirely right; the article shall be sent to my house immediately; but let me ask your aid in selecting books of the kind you recommend." Rather, I answered, let me sketch for you a course of reading, embracing a view of the various departments of literature with which you will need to become gradually acquainted, and leave you to fill up the case at your leisure, according to your sense of want, and the demands for knowledge which various occasions will urge upon you.

Thus arose before my mind the ideal form of a family library exhibited in the following pages. It will be seen, therefore, that in developing it, I address myself to those who have something to do besides reading. I speak to those who have a business which demands their attention, but who, feeling the importance of mental improvement, can manage to devote three or four hours every day to this purpose. I address those who are not too far advanced in life to lay out for themselves a *course of reading*, which, though they may daily glance as much as need be at newspapers and ephemeral publications, they will yet pursue through a succession of years, believing that it embraces the elements of a mental culture which will repay their labors in manifold and ever-spreading harvests of wisdom and happiness.

Evidently, it would not accord with such a design to name all the good books, or even all the best, which one might think of in each department. I must keep in view the size of the young man's book-case, and the limits of his time, if not of his purse. By means of as few books as possible, I would aid him in obtaining that information which is essential to self-culture, and in becoming naturalized to that realm of polite and useful knowledge where the intelligent of all lands meet as on common ground, and in some sort commune together as a common brotherhood.

First of all, then, the book which more than one learned German writer has called "the primitive document of the human race,"*—the book of which Coleridge has well said, "to give its literary history would be little less than to relate the origin and first excitement of all the literature and science which we now possess,"†—the book which is composed of many works, historical, doctrinal, ethical, and poetical, written by various authors, through a range of sixteen hundred years, and which, since its completion, has moulded the character and swayed the opinions of the civilized world,—the book whose moral power over social man is yet in its early process of development, —the book which, from its acknowledged preëminence, is by universal consent called THE BIBLE, puts forth such kingly claims on our attention, that the first division of a course of reading should undoubtedly be,

THE BIBLICAL DEPARTMENT.

I mention the Bible first on account of its intrinsic dignity as a revelation from Heaven, and also on account of its connection with every sphere of duty and every branch of knowledge. Its name may be truly called "wonderful." It has been the well-spring of every influence which has wrought a beneficial change in the social condition of mankind. The Vedas, the Shasters, and Korans of the Eastern world have kept

* Schlegel, Philos. of Hist., p. 191. † Lit. Biog., chap. 11.

the nations subject to them fixed in the bondage of their old opinions, their superstitions, and their ignorance; but if on a map of the globe you draw a line around those countries which are distinguished by knowledge, by civilization, and the triumphs of scientific art, you will have encircled Christendom. It is true, indeed, that after the Roman Empire with its ancient civilization had been swept away, and Huns, Goths, and Vandals, had made Europe a desolation those barbarians received Christianity in a weak and corrupted form; among their descendants the Scriptures were but little understood, church pomps and ceremonies engrossed the mind, and the priest interposed between God and the soul which he had made. In the best portions of Europe, society did sink, we readily admit, below the level of its condition in Mohammedan countries. But in the midst of that darkness, the moral power of the Bible became manifest; for when brought out to the light, translated into the common language, and circulated among the people, it developed those energies which have set forward the Christian nations upon a career of improvement, so far in advance of all those idolaters who inhabit Asia and Africa.

The Bible is the most *suggestive* book that was ever written. Search the libraries of the Old or the New World, and you will find that some of the most costly offerings laid on the shrine of literature have been essays, discourses, or treatises, suggested by texts of Scripture. Often, a single sentence has set on fire some mighty genius, as a Newton, a Boyle, a Butler, or a

Hall, and quickened into life their dormant energies. If then, one chance to feel himself hard pressed by the cares of business, let him not slight this book on that account. If he have opportunity to read a newspaper, or take a repast, let him also turn one reverent glance towards the Bible; for a single line drawn from such a portion as the Sermon on the Mount may come home to his bosom amid the snares and hurry of the day, laden with the richest blessings.

One charm of the Bible is this: that while many a short phrase of it may rouse a child or a man to profitable thought, and while the whole work may be carried in your pocket, biblical literature is ever putting forth new attractions, expanding itself before you, like a field whose surface yields the finest fruits, and whose depths are stored with costly ores and gems. To explore it is a work worthy of a good share of any lifetime. After a general acquaintance with the Bible, a superficial reading will probably excite but little interest, but an earnest and daily study of it will move the deepest springs of thought and feeling in the soul.

In order to study it with success, some helps are desirable. Of these, the most necessary is a CONCORDANCE, which saves much useless labor in finding passages, only one word of which may be accurately remembered. Next to this in importance is a Commentary, or book of explanatory and practical notes. In aids of this sort, for general use, our religious literature has always been rather poor. There are numerous commentaries adapted to the student's closet, or the library of the parish minister, but few there are which present those clear, brief statements of the sense of a passage, so much needed by the family circle or the general reader. MATTHEW HENRY and DOCTOR SCOTT, the most popular of all the writers of this class, are excellent in their way, but it seems to have been their design to *lecture* to us from a paragraph, rather than to furnish those simple annotations which would give the inquirer a clue to the meaning of the sacred text. In many cases, therefore, where their help is most requisite, they yield us none. ADAM CLARKE was more learned than either of these, and his work, as to its plan, better realizes the true idea of a Commentary; but he fails to adhere to sound principles of interpretation, and is often as fanciful as a Jewish Rabbi in his views of the sense of his author. Dr. GILL, like Clarke, is rich in learning, but for most readers is too voluminous; occupying much space in showing what a sentence does *not* mean, and illustrates too copiously from Rabbinical authorities. Other authors might be named, whose works are excellent as aids to the theological student, or as suggestors of devotional and practical thought, but quite defective in that kind of elucidation desired by the generality of readers. Of late years, a new class of commentaries have been issued, and they mark the era of great improvement. To the Sabbath-school Institution belongs the honor of giving them birth, for the weekly demands of some hundred thousands of Sabbath-school teachers, learning in order to communicate, have been the occasion of their existence. BARNES' Notes are constructed on a plan admirably adapted to general use, and are most deserving of a place in a family library. It is to be hoped that in due time they will embrace the whole of the Old, as well as the New Testament. BUSH'S Commentary on the Pentateuch is the best popular annotation on that most ancient and important part of Scripture, and unaffected by those doubtful principles of interpretation which appear in some of his later writings. RIPLEY on the Gospels furnishes a fine specimen of sound criticism, but he is rather too concise. On the Acts of the Apostles, however, the only inspired history of the Christian Church, "Ripley's Notes" are the most perfect model of a popular commentary ever published, being written in a beautifully transparent style, illuminating what is obscure, never trenching on the province of a sermon or lecture, and avoiding either extreme of redundance or conciseness.

Now let any one peruse a few verses of the Scripture in regular order, day by day, availing himself of the lights which such comments furnish,—let him reflect on the whole until he thoroughly penetrate the meaning of the writer, withal devoutly asking Divine assistance, and to him the Bible will never grow old, or pall the sense, but will be ever fresh as if its leaves had just been dropped from the skies, fragrant with celestial dews, and bright with the inscriptions of a seraph's pen.

II. The next portion of the Family Library which claims attention is the

POLITICAL DEPARTMENT.

Of this division, there would be but slight incentives to speak at all in any country except America, for nowhere else does every family embrace those whose relations to their country involve such grave responsibilities as men and citizens. Here only, the people are really self-governed; here only, the high and the low, the rich and the poor, possess equal weight in the scale of political rule; who, then, can over-estimate the moral and religious responsibilities which cluster around the head of him who has received the boon of American citizenship? Although very few volumes may suffice to answer the end of this department, yet these are quite indispensable. One or more books developing the Constitution of the United States, the structure and operations of the Government, should be in the hands of every man who holds the right of suffrage, or every woman who can influence those who wield it.

Chief among this class of works stands STORY'S COMMENTARIES ON THE CONSTITUTION. The original publication was in three volumes; but there is a beautiful abridgment by the author, for the use of school libraries and general readers. TOCQUEVILLE'S DEMOCRACY IN AMERICA exhibits many broad views and profound lessons, deserving the study of every young man. The same remark may justly be made of the FEDERALIST, by HAMILTON, MADISON, and JAY, in one volume. If any one, however, would fain satisfy himself with a small book, as a manual of principles and duties, he may obtain "YOUNG'S SCIENCE OF GOVERNMENT," published at Rochester, New York. SULLIVAN'S POLITICAL CLASS BOOK also contains a great amount of information which ought to be more widely diffused. And as it is evident that without some knowledge of political economy, a people may ignorantly oppose the very measures which would conduce to the public welfare, such books on that subject as those of SAY, WAYLAND, and ADAM SMITH'S Wealth of Nations, deserve a prominent place in a plan of home-reading. WAYLAND'S abridgment of his Political Economy is a pocket volume for the young, admirably adapted to its purpose.

A popular interest in the science of political economy is a clear sign of the progress of Christian civilization. It is remarked by Condorcet, and after him, by Dugald Stewart, that in the sixteenth century the science of political economy did not exist. Princes estimated not the number of men, but of soldiers in the state; finance was the art of plundering the people without driving them to the desperation of revolt and government paid no other attention to commerce than that of loading it with taxes, of restricting it by privileges, or of disputing for its monopoly. Similar to this is a statement of Mr. Hume, "that there is scarcely any ancient writer on politics who has made mention of trade, nor was it ever considered an affair of state until the seventeenth century." The celebrated Dutch statesman, John DeWitt, was the first author who ever published any thing of note on this subject in connection with politics; and while in other lands it is deemed sufficient if the rulers themselves understand this subject, here, certainly, the knowledge of its general principles should be almost universal.

III.—The third class of books which now commend themselves to us, belong to the department of history.

After obtaining a general knowledge of the history of our own country, such as is usually obtained in the public schools, two courses propose themselves to our choice. We can either read the history of those nations from which we sprang, then of those connected with their origin, and so travel backward to the earliest times, or we can begin at once with ancient history and come down by degrees to our own age. I far prefer the latter course; because it seems to me that thus the events will be more naturally associated in the order of time, and will be more at the command of the memory. Some, however, choose the former, on account of its awakening, as they think, a deeper interest in the story. The historical course which I am about to suggest, is the very *shortest* that I can think of, as adapted to answer the end of an inquiring reader, and yet, if well pursued, will enable one with advantage to strike forth laterally in any direction whither his curiosity may lead him.

The best beginning which one can make in this department, is to select good *compends*, which, while they map out the field of history, and show the extent of the study, are yet composed with such graphic power as to awaken an interest in the characters and fortunes of men and of nations. A compend consisting of dry details is very easily made, but it can be of very little use to a beginner; to write a history of compendious brevity so as to throw a charm around the story, is a work requiring the highest skill. Two authors have done this successfully. The first is ROLLIN, whose ancient history of the Egyptians, Carthaginians, Assyrians, Babylonians, Medes and Persians, and Greeks, is one of the most beautiful offerings ever laid upon the shrine of popular literature. The second is GOLDSMITH, whose abridged history of Rome has the attractions of a romance. I have known nice critics who spoke lightly of these works; but it was clear to me in every case, that although their knowledge of particular periods was accurate and minute, yet they were deficient themselves in that *comprehensive* knowledge of history which they would have possessed, had they commenced their reading in the manner just mentioned.*

* Sometimes very just remarks which seem to depreciate Rollins' history, are only intended to bear on those who are indisposed to go beyond his work for information. Thus, Mr. Hume, writing to Dr. Robertson on the difficulties in the way of any one's composing a history of Greece successfully, makes this observation: "Besides, Rollin is so well wrote with respect to style, that with superficial people it passes for sufficient." This criticism, however, pays a tacit compliment to Rollin's work, when viewed in the light of a compend.

In this letter from which I have quoted, there is a remark of Mr. Hume which furnishes an argument for the course which I am recommending, of reading the translations of the old historians. Hume is endeavoring to dissuade Robertson from risking his reputation on a history of Greece, and says: "The ancient Greek history has several recommendations, particularly the good authors from which it must be drawn; but this same circumstance becomes an objection, when more narrowly considered; for what can you do in most places with these authors, but transcribe and translate them? No letters or state-papers from which you could correct their errors,

After mastering these compends, it is best to proceed at once to the writers whose works form the *sources* of history, and who, from their proximity to the characters and events which they describe, are distinguished by a higher degree of life, spirit, and naturalness, than can be found in any modern author treating the same subjects. What though they have not written in our own language? If we cannot read the originals, why should we refuse to avail ourselves of the translations? Who does not know that many a traveller through Palestine, familiar from youth with his English Bible, has found every hill and vale, every lake, and stream, and tree, and shrub, most dear in its associations, although he could not read one word of Hebrew? By means of these versions we may transport ourselves to distant scenes, and feel ourselves to be in companionship with men of ancient generations. Instead, then, of consuming more time on modern writers of ancient history, turn to the father of secular history, and read HERODOTUS; then THUCYDIDES, on the Peloponnesian war; XENOPHON'S Greek History, and POLYBIUS' History of the Greeks and Romans from the commencement of the second Punic war to the downfall of Perseus, the last king of Macedon. Follow these with LIVY, whose graphic power has never been excelled; TACITUS, remarkable for conciseness; SALLUST'S History of the war with Jugurtha and Cataline's conspiracy, together with JULIUS CÆSAR'S

---

or authenticate their narration, or supply their defects."—*Dugald Stewart's Life and Writings of Dr. Robertson, p.* 121.

Commentaries, or Journal of his Wars, which, by the way, will be a capital introduction to the History of France, England, Switzerland, and Germany. Good English versions of these histories have long since been given to the world, and the American public has received from the prolific press of the Harpers, pocket editions of most or all of them.

Next to these, would properly come the European history of a thousand years, which has been written with success only by a man who has occasionally interwoven somewhat of his subtle scepticism with the story, and bearing the celebrated title, GIBBON'S History of the Decline and Fall of the Roman Empire. It is a work which could never have been written on this continent, nor anywhere else, except in the neighborhood of those immense old libraries which are the fountains of historic knowledge. Its execution required a man of learning and of fortune, and the command of twenty years' leisure, all of which its author possessed. It bridges over the chasm between ancient and modern history, and enables us to pass with even pace and with a continuity of impression, from the perusal of the Roman to that of the English writers.

At this stage of the course, the reader may take up with advantage, PRESCOTT'S history of Ferdinand and Isabella, which presents a vivid picture of the state of Europe in the age which was signalized by the discovery of America. This should be followed by ROBERTSON'S history of Charles V., Emperor of Germany, who became heir to the crown of Spain, not omitting the Introduction, which gives a broad and clear retrospective view of the condition of Europe. With a master's hand Dr. Robertson has pictured forth the political relations of the European kingdoms and states at the opening of the sixteenth century. It is a great work, and at first seemed to be attended with so many difficulties, that Mr. Hume, in a friendly correspondence, urged the author not to undertake it; but, fortunately for mankind, Dr. Robertson consulted his own judgment.

With the general knowledge of the Old World now acquired, it may be well to study more minutely the history of England, by reading, at first, GOLDSMITH'S brief history, following it with KEIGHTLEY, or going directly to HUME and SMOLLETT. The brilliant volumes of MACAULAY, however, will be read with a keen zest by every one who is interested in those periods of English history which have been illustrated by his pictorial pen.

Of the history of France there is an excellent compend by Mrs. JAMIESON. GOODRICH'S Pictorial History of France will also answer well the purpose of a compend. If it be practicable, it would be a good economy of time, to read after the outline-history, the article on France in the *Encyclopædia Britannica.* MICHELET'S history of France has, of late years, supplied an urgent want. A similar remark is applicable to the history of the Revolution, by THIERS; and the history of modern Europe by ALISON, notwithstanding his high-toned, bigoted conservatism, cannot well be spared from the historical department of a family library. Every reader must learn to make due allowance for the political, the religious, or the irreligious prejudices of authors.

Time was when Asiatic history was almost entirely neglected amongst us. But of late years, Turkey, Hindostan, and China have been attracting anew the attention of Europe and America. On this account, such works as ROBERTSON'S India, GUTZLAFF'S China, and MAVOR'S Ottoman Empire in Asia, deserve a special mention. A knowledge of the Old World acquired in a course of reading projected somewhat in this line of direction, will prepare one to approach with a keen zest, and a power of just appreciation, the history of America.

In this department the best works are of recent origin, except ROBERTSON'S History of America, which is beautifully written, and, with all its imperfections, will amply repay a careful perusal. BANCROFT'S History of the United States is not yet completed; but the six volumes already issued must be always considered as an indispensable part of an American's library, however strongly he may dissent from some opinions therein expressed. Far from being a mere summary of events, it is the history of the leading ideas,—a development of the mind and heart of a nation. GRAHAME'S History of the United States from the colonial settlements to the War of Independence is also a valuable acquisition to the list of works on America, although it contains several important errors. The author was a Scotchman by birth, but an American in heart; and chiefly derived the materials of his history neither from America nor from England, but from the libraries of Germany! It is a remarkable fact that BOTTA, an Italian, has written the best history of the American Revolution ever published. Had he been acquainted with all the leaders of the war, had he been an eye-witness of all its scenes, he could scarcely have described them with more of vivacity and truthfulness. His work has been translated by Geo. Alex. Otis, Esq., of Boston. It is a fine compliment which GRAHAME has paid to BOTTA in saying that he had intended to write the history of the American War, but that, on reading the Italian's work, he had abandoned the project altogether.

In addition to these great works on the rise, progress, and fall of nations, the family library should contain some means of information on the subjects of Ecclesiastical History. If only one work can be afforded, and that of the smaller class, I would unite with the Rev. John Angell James in recommending JONES'S "History of the Christian Church from the Birth of Christ to the Beginning of the Eighteenth Century." MOSHEIM'S Church History is a larger work, a standard authority, and extensively read; yet it is written too much in the style of a dry compend, and the narrative is broken by the division into centuries. NEANDER'S History of the Church is the greatest and the best production of the present age in this department. The History of Christianity by MILMAN, one of the most learned writers of the Church of England, is a work composed with the highest skill, and comprises a vast amount of information and of just reflection within a narrow space. D'AUBIGNE'S History of the Reformation no reader in this department would be disposed to omit; and in connection with it, one may profitably read FATHER PAUL'S History of the Council of Trent, which Bishop Burnet pronounced one of the finest models of historic composition that the world has seen.

To any one who shall be engaged in pursuing this course of historical reading, Dr. TAYLOR'S Manual of Ancient and Modern History* may be of immense service in presenting a panoramic view of the diversified scene which he is aiming to traverse; and he who shall have pursued this course deliberately, will find that all the parts of his historical knowledge are intimately connected, and that they bear the impress of unity. Such a knowledge of the civilized world will well repay the labor that it costs; and, as we have wished to reach it by one of the shortest paths, we have forborne to name some of the noblest works in the realm of History. These will present themselves to the student's view as he advances. Let him, if he please, notice the number of writers referred to by Gibbon, Robertson, Prescott, and Bancroft, and he will see how widely he may extend his researches. And here, if conciseness, if *condensation* be earnestly sought by the young reader, let me say to him with a special emphasis, that whosoever shall thoroughly master the works of these four last-named writers—Gibbon, Robertson, Prescott, Bancroft, may be fairly regarded

---

* An American edition has been published by Appleton, with a chapter on the History of the United States, by Rev. C. S. Henry, D D.

as a well-informed man, and will rarely, if ever, be at a loss, or placed at a serious disadvantage, in the society of highly learned and cultivated men. Brief as this historical course may seem to some, he who does it justice practically will find himself able to trace the origin of nations, to revolve in his mind the great events which have distinguished the annals of our race, to mark the slow and sure development of a grand scheme of Divine Providence, moving onward with majestic force to some wondrous consummation; and if he be a man of genuine Christian principle, while he deplores the follies and the miseries of his species, he will be incited to task himself the more earnestly for the promotion of that celestial kingdom which embraces within itself the fortunes of humanity, and which, like the little stone that the prophet saw come forth from the mountain-side, is destined to gather new accessions of grandeur, to crush all forms of opposition in its way, and to fill the world with its enduring strength and glory.

IV. The fourth class of books in our course of reading, belongs to the department of

BIOGRAPHY.

The late Dr. Arnold called history, according to his view of what it ought to be, "the biography of a nation." This is a good statement of the true aim of history. And as a nation is composed of individuals, it will be found that the biography of distinguished persons represents in a great degree the life of a nation or an age. It is true, there are some who live before their time; who, becoming possessed of some great truth, unwelcome to their generation, feel themselves impelled to become its heralds, to conquer as its champions, or die as its martyrs. Such an one was ARNOLD OF BRESCIA, whose ashes were mingled with the waters of the Tiber, for proclaiming as a Christian doctrine the rightful separation of the government of the church from that of the state; such men were COPERNICUS and GALILEO, who were imprisoned for teaching the revolution of the earth around the sun; such a man was JOHN HUSS, who amidst the flames of death predicted the triumph of his cause. This class of men do not represent their nation; they are prophets of the future; they represent *ideas*, which, struggling for mastery, become the property of succeeding times. Biographies of the great, therefore, may be divided into two classes: first, the memoirs of individuals who struggle for some great truth *against* their age; the second comprising memoirs of those who embody the spirit of their age. To the first class belongs VAUGHN'S LIFE OF WYCLIFFE, whose course on earth was a contest for one glorious truth—the supremacy of God's Word. The Life and Times of LUTHER and of MELANCTHON, who struggled for the great doctrine of Justification by a living Faith instead of dead ceremonies; the Life of ROGER WILLIAMS, who embodied the clear conception of the universal right of man to religious liberty as an essential element of Christianity; the lives of all those of whom the Church of England in her service makes touching mention in those well-known words, "the noble army of martyrs praise thee!" To the second class belong The Life of Cicero, by Dr. MIDDLETON, a capital work; LANGHORNE'S Translation of Plutarch's Lives; Memoirs of Sully; JOHNSON'S Lives of the Poets; BOSWELL'S Life of Johnson; CARLYLE'S Life of Cromwell;* LORD BROUGHAM'S Statesmen of the Reign of George III.; SPARKS' American Biography; for these portray the leading statesmen, scholars, orators, and poets, whose names were potent with the world, and whose characters were impressed on the popular mind of their own age. Such biographies are identified with the history of mankind, and display at once the fortunes of the race and the traits of individual history.

V. To the fifth department of our library we assign

BOOKS OF TRAVELS.

The most important of this class are those which have been written within our own times, or a comparatively recent period. For history and biography exhibit to us the world as it *has been;* but we need a knowledge of the world as it *is now;* and for this we must resort to the accounts of those who have described what they have seen. There never was an age so rich as is the present in information of this kind; the speed of communication, and the spirit of the missionary enterprise, having combined to fulfil the ancient prediction, "many shall run to and fro, and knowledge shall increase in the earth."

It is quite remarkable how much the writings of

* See Note A. Oliver Cromwell.

missionaries have added to our stock of general information respecting the world at large. Their accounts, too, are more to be relied on than were those of the majority of travellers in former times. The readers of their journals are somewhat in advance of the rest of society in their knowledge of other nations. Of this truth we have seen a practical illustration. A few years since, the American Embassy to China, on returning home, politely acknowledged its indebtedness to Dr. Parker, a missionary of the American Board, for the intelligence which he communicated, and for his services as interpreter. The Secretary of Legation, Fletcher Webster, Esq., favored the public in our principal cities with lectures on China. Those who had opportunities of judging in the case were struck with the observation, that to those portions of each audience who were not familiar with missionary writings the statements of the lecturer possessed an air of startling and romantic novelty, while, on the other hand, those accustomed to read their books and journals heard little that astonished them, and could verify the assertions of the speaker.

To those who are about to become travellers themselves, it is generally known that the guide-book of MADAME STARKE is the great repository of practical information for European tourists. But it is not of much service in one's library until he shall have used it abroad; then it becomes richly associated with vivid reminiscences.

But that knowledge of other lands which one may advantageously obtain from books at home, can be found by consulting such authors as the following: HENDERSON'S Biblical Researches and Travels in Russia; BAIRD'S Northern Europe; STEVENS' Travels in Greece, Turkey, Russia, and Poland—a book of extraordinary ease and charm of manner; France, by HENRY L. BULWER, M. P.; Spain, by Hon. CALEB CUSHING; also a later work on Spain, by WALLIS; BORROW'S Bible in Spain—one of the most fascinating of books; FORSYTH'S Remarks on Italy; MARIANNE BAILLIE'S Sketches of the Manners and Customs of Portugal. On Asia, only a few books need be mentioned here. HOWARD MALCOM'S Travels in Hindustan, Malaya, Siam, and China, with a full account of the Burman Empire, is a book possessing a well-established character for breadth and accuracy of observation. It has been hailed with a welcome from all quarters. ABEEL'S Residence in China, GUTZLAFF'S Voyages, Sir A. BURNES'S Travels up the Indus, FRAZER'S Journey across the Himalaya Mountains, and WILSON'S Travels in the Holy Land, Egypt, &c., present a just and lively picture of Asiatic life as it is in our own day.

On Africa, a most entertaining book is "The Lights and Shadows of African History," in Peter Parley's Cabinet Library. Let no one despise it because it is gotten up in a style which addresses itself to the curiosity of youth. That little book, together with its companions in the set, condense a vast amount of reading, and must have cost a great deal of labor. A larger, graver work is the Historical Account of Discoveries and Travels in Africa, from the earliest ages to the present time, by HUGH MURRAY, Esq. 2 vols. octavo. 1818. Mr. MOFFATT's book on the African Mission, with which he had been long connected, is one of thrilling interest. SMITH and CHOULES's History of Missions is, to some extent, a book of travels in Africa, as well as other parts, and combines, in many instances, the grave air of narrative with an attraction like that of romance. BAYARD TAYLOR, in his late work on Africa, has made a valuable addition to this department of literature.

GRUND's Travels in the United States is one of the best books of the sort on this country. LYELL's Book of Travels is the best specimen of just and lively description by an English tourist, and CHEVALIER's Letters, published a dozen years ago, will enable an American to see his own country from an intelligent Frenchman's point of view.

STEVENS's Travels in Central America is full of novel incidents. MACGILLIVRAY's Digest of Baron Humboldt's Travels, chiefly in South America, (Harpers' edition,) is a work of rare excellence for the amount of information condensed into a narrow space.

A general view of this department of our literature at the present day, of the characters and objects of the writers, will lead us to indulge a pleasing train of reflections, after reading the following remarks, which fell more than half a century ago from the pen of Dr. Johnson: "The Europeans have scarcely visited any coast but to gratify avarice and extend corruption; to arrogate dominion without right, and practise cruelty without incentive. Much knowledge has been acquired, and much cruelty been committed; the belief of religion has been very little propagated, and its laws have been outrageously and enormously violated; but there is reason to hope that out of so much evil good may some time be produced, and that the light of the gospel will at last illuminate the sands of Africa, the deserts of America, though its progress cannot but be slow, when it is so much obstructed by the lives of Christians."

VI. To the sixth class of books in the Family Library, belong

Works of Imagination.

There is a fine critical remark of that splendid reviewer, Macaulay, which, though once it would have been heard with a sneer, now expresses the opinion of the world. It is this: "Though there were many clever men in England during the latter half of the seventeenth century, there were only two great creative minds. One of those minds produced the Paradise Lost, the other the Pilgrim's Progress."* A preceding age, however, had seen one other such mind, whose productions were chiefly dramas. In the realm of English literature, these three, SHAKSPEARE, MILTON, BUNYAN, are now enthroned as extraordinary beings, endowed with creative genius. They are a trio of crowned heads. The brow of each is imperial.

Among works of imagination, then, the three productions just mentioned hold the first rank. So widely

* Edinburgh Review, No. CVIII., 1831. Last words of the Review of Southey's edition of the Pilgrim's Progress.

are they known, that the allusions of English literature cannot now be understood without our having read them. Of Shakspeare, however, let it be said, that he should be *studied* rather than read. With how many is his name popular who do not understand him! But one of the brightest signs of mental and social progress which has appeared within a few years past, is the fact that so many thousands prefer to read Shakspeare by the fireside, or listen to profound critical lectures upon his dramas, to seeing them represented in action on a stage. How well worthy of notice is it, that multitudes whom the theatre had ceased to charm, have gone evening after evening to hear Mr. Hudson's lectures on Shakspeare, and even to hear Shaksperean readings. And undoubtedly it is true that the more intelligent and refined a community become, the more perfect and exalted will be their ideals of heroic character, the more impatient of a defective representation, the less dependent on the outward show and stir of action for an impression of it, the better able to enjoy their own vivid conceptions which are awakened by a calm and noiseless reading, the more in love with that quiet mood of mind which brings one into communion with the spirit of a profound dramatic author, who in his closet lived for awhile all absorbed in those scenes which at last he pictured forth in plastic language, expressed in flowing verse, and made the printed page seem radiant with a glory almost supernatural.

For the first reading of Milton, it would be well, if possible, to procure an edition with DR. NEWTON'S Notes, or JOHNSON'S, chiefly selected from Newton.

SCOTT'S Notes on the Pilgrim's Progress are often valuable, and CHEEVER'S Lectures, lately published, is worthy of its popularity. Dr. Johnson said that there were only two or three books in the world that he had wished longer, and of these the Pilgrim's Progress was one. "It was by no common merit," says Macaulay, "that the illiterate sectary extracted praise like this from the most pedantic of critics and the most bigoted of tories."

Beyond the place occupied by these three kingly works, the domain of English poetry is very ample. To the most cursory observer its productions would seem to be enough to fill the space ordinarily assigned to a family library. Numerous and varied as they are, some may ask, How shall we select those best qualified to claim our "Poet's Corner?" It might be difficult in a few words or lines to give an answer to this question which the judgment of every reader would ratify; but the two elegant volumes of RUFUS W. GRISWOLD, on the Poets and Poetry of England and America, containing those productions of each writer which exhibit his traits of character most advantageously, will enable their possessor to survey at once the wide realm of the English or American muse, and will supply him with those pleasing contrasts which are adapted to cultivate his taste and to sharpen his powers of discrimination. A similar remark is applicable to CHAMBERS' Cyclopædia of English Literature, (Gould and Lincoln's edition,) which fills a wider space, embracing the prose-writers as well as the poets, from the rude remains of Anglo-Saxon authors to the more polished works of our own day. The brief historical notices with which these volumes abound, render them a valuable accession to our literature.

Although the study of *English* poetry is the most important to us, as far as the end of poetry is concerned, yet the translations of foreign poets deserve a share of our attention. The chief means of cultivating a good poetic taste is the same as should be employed in regard to painting, or any other sphere of art; that is, comparison. English versions, therefore, of the Greek, Roman, and Italian poets, will aid one much in attaining this object, and will also quicken our interest in history, by bringing us closer to the daily life, the homes and the hearts of the ancients. COWPER'S HOMER, POTTER'S ÆSCHYLUS AND EURIPIDES, DALE'S SOPHOCLES, DR. FRANCIS'S HORACE, DRYDEN'S VIRGIL, and LUCAN'S PHARSALIA by ROWE, will well repay a rapid glance or a closer inspection. The great Italian poet, whose name is associated with Milton's, may be read in CAREY'S translation; but a superior version of the first ten cantos of DANTE has been made by our young countryman, T. W. PARSONS, of Boston. It were to be wished that he might be encouraged and stimulated to complete what he has begun. PETRARCH'S ARIOSTO has been fairly translated by HOOLE, and TASSO'S JERUSALEM DELIVERED has been elegantly translated by FAIRFAX; and he who reads this latter poem will be rewarded by high enjoyment as he proceeds, and by the opportunity of judging for himself whether Dryden and Voltaire were right in pronouncing it the first epic of modern times.

The mighty influence of poetry over the minds of men, its power to quicken the higher faculties and the finer sensibilities of the soul, has been universally acknowledged. In regard to the effects of prose fiction, considered as a whole, there has been a difference of opinion. Perhaps this may be accounted for by the fact, that this latter kind of writing is so generally looked at "in the gross;" and inasmuch as many presses have incessantly teemed with that trashy, sentimental, sensual class of publications, which pass under the name of "novels," these have often filled the whole sphere of vision when one has been speaking of prose fiction. But why should works of imagination, when written in prose, be treated of in the mass, and judged without discrimination, any more than when written in verse? There have been poems as bad as novels, produced by, and addressed to, the same mental faculties and susceptibilities. Are poems, therefore, to be condemned as such? Not all: but in regard to them, as to many other things in this state of probation, we must have "our senses exercised to discern both good and evil." Works of imagination are founded on the essential nature of man—have always existed, and must exist for ever. And as long as the world contains so many idlers and loungers as it does, who resort to a book for the same reason as they do to a play or a game of cards, merely "to kill time," or for a sport of fancy, there will be writers to cater for their diseased appetites. But, just as the way to prevent or cure intoxication, is not to destroy all the alcohol or opium from off the earth, but to cultivate right habits of self-direction; so, the true way to guard against mental revelry, is, not to proscribe all works of imagination, but to form a taste quick to discern between the precious and the vile; to "take the good, and cast the bad away."

Without doubt, there is danger of abuse; but where are we not liable to this? The first, the necessary evil of a careless, indiscriminate reading of this class of works, is well expressed in a single line by Hannah More:

> "They add fresh strength to what was strong before."

It destroys the mental balance, and gives to the imagination an undue predominance. Instead of acting in harmony with the other faculties, and becoming auxiliary to their improvement and expansion, it usurps their place, exhausts their energy, and smites them with a sort of moral palsy. Sad havoc does it make of the intellectual taste; for it sickens of all reality, and craves only that which is analogous to the narcotics and stimulants of the pampered epicure.

The real good to be derived from works of imagination is analogous to the benefit which we derive from visiting a gallery of pictures from the hands of true masters. These aid our conceptions of truth in the world of nature and reality. He who has gazed on such a work of art as Belshazzar's Feast, by Allston; the Last Supper, by Da Vinci; or the Battle of Constantine, by Raphael, feels conscious of mental elevation, and blesses genius for having stooped to aid him, for having brought the past and the distant near him, and enabled him to behold more clearly the scenes and characters, the men and the events, of other lands and ages. Thus, he who has pored over the pages of SIR WALTER SCOTT'S KENILWORTH or PEVERIL OF THE PEAK, where the actions of other times are presented before him as in a lively panorama, experiences emotions of healthful pleasure akin to those which swell the bosom of the traveller when he is ushered into the scenes and associations of a foreign country where the manners, customs, language, features, gait, and costume, of which he had but faintly conceived, are around him as parts of the actual world and of real life.

Never did an author universally popular apprehend and reach the proper end of this class of writings, considered as works of art, like Sir Walter Scott. His influence on the taste of the present generation has been vast and salutary; a counterpoise to much that is low and degrading in the realm of fiction, and a preventive of much that, but for him, would have been encouraged to court the popular favor. However much his political prejudices may have unduly tinged som of his historical portraits, he is ever to be honored as a benefactor of his race.

Having formed a clear idea of the true *design* of works which belong to this department of literature, any one may easily select for himself those which are in accordance with it. It does not belong to my plan to enumerate them here. Suffice it to say, that all of JAMES'S historical romances, if found to be entertaining, will be very instructive; that DEFOE'S ROBINSON

CRUSOE should be read as the author published it, and not in an abridgment; that GOLDSMITH'S "Vicar of Wakefield" should not be supplanted by any modern work of its class; that "Happiness," by ANDREW REED, D. D., is a good picture of true religion amidst the snares of fashion; and that some of the leading minds of the present day are more indebted for the religious bias of their characters to "Father Clement," than to all the volumes of learning and argument which they had ever seen.

VII. A seventh division of the Family Library, however small it may be, should be reserved for a few works on

INTELLECTUAL AND MORAL PHILOSOPHY.

It is impossible to give an adequate idea of the worth of this department to any one whose attention has not been directed to it, or one who has experienced no benefit from it. I have known professional and practical men who attributed their success in life, in a high degree, to the knowledge and the mental discipline acquired by reading carefully one or two books on these subjects; and have received the most cordial thanks from some whom I have urged to study at least a single work. A clear view of the faculties of the mind, of what it is capable of accomplishing, of the prejudices to which it is liable, the mode of analyzing its operations and governing it effectively, the errors to be guarded against in its cultivation, the nature of reasoning, the limits of human knowledge, the grounds and laws of belief, can not be too highly prized by any class of men.

If time and circumstances allowed one but a single book on intellectual philosophy, I should give PROFESSOR UPHAM'S Elements a decided preference. It is an admirable *map* of the science. The references under each chapter will aid the reader in pursuing any subject within its scope. Next to this I would take DUGALD STEWART'S Elements of Mental Philosophy. If any one however should design a thorough study of this department, he should begin with LOCKE'S ESSAY, the first book, with twelve chapters of the second; for hence have sprung the discussions which have employed the writers and the schools of Europe for the last half century.

DUGALD STEWART'S Dissertation on the Progress of Metaphysical, Ethical, and Political Philosophy since the revival of learning in Europe, is worthy of being obtained by any effort that it might require. It forms the sixth volume of the Cambridge edition of his works.

WAYLAND'S Moral Philosophy is generally acknowledged to be the best treatise on this subject for the use of a student.

VIII. To the last division of our library we refer that class of writings which usually pass under the name of "Miscellanies," embracing Essays, Discourses, Dissertations, and Treatises on various subjects, and which constitute the bulk of the English classics. For the heads and representatives of these we must find room. They touch all themes, and exhibit every variety of style. Lord Bacon observes that treatises require leisure; and that as of that he had but little, he wrote essays. He adds, "The word is late, but the thing is ancient; for Seneca's Epistles to Lucilius, if you mark them well, are but *Essays*, that is, dispersed meditations, though conveyed in the form of epistles." A similar remark may be applied to modern Reviews, which appear in the form, now of an essay, like Channing's Milton, now of a dissertation or argumentative discussion, and now again of a treatise or methodical development of a subject. The productions of BACON, ADDISON, JOHNSON, ROBERT HALL, JOHN FOSTER, WAYLAND, MACAULAY, WILSON, IRVING, WILLIAMS,* and WHIPPLE,† are moulding character and opinion wherever the English language has been understood. Other names are already associated with this noble host; may many more arise to join them, to do still better for the generations yet to come, and make our English literature a blessing wide as the world and enduring as the human race.

PLAN OF READING.

In addition to these suggestions on a course of reading, a few words on the plan of pursuing it may not be amiss. There is good reason to believe that the example of Dr. Johnson, who is often spoken of as having been a great desultory reader, choosing his book from impulse and accident, then laying it aside ere it was finished, has had an injurious influence on the mental habits of many a young man. Such a practice might do very well for that renowned critic, who oc-

---

* See Note B. Literature of the Pulpit.

† See Note C. Whipple's Lectures.

cupied an eminence whence the whole domain of literature lay spread out to his view; who had in his mind, to use a common phrase, "a place for every thing, and every thing in its place." By a cursory reading he could easily take the bearings of an author, scan him thoroughly, analyze, and classify him. Great as was his genius, however, before he could do this, his reading had extended far beyond the limits of a family library. His example therefore is not to be recommended to one who has not pursued such a course of reading as will make him familiar with those standard works which in relation to general knowledge, are to be considered as initial and elementary. The young reader may hope to see the day when he shall be able to use and enjoy books as Dr. Johnson did; but to begin at the outset to imitate his habits in this respect, would be as unfortunate, though not as ridiculous, as some writers have appeared to be, who, with little practice, like dwarfs on stilts, have essayed to imitate his style.

It is absolutely necessary for any one who would gain available information, to read, for a while at least, somewhat continuously. However short the time of each day that he may be able to command, let him read a few verses of the Scripture with such comments as may explain or enforce its meaning. If he were not disposed to do this from principle, as a Christian, yet if he do it not at all, he will be greatly the loser as a scholar.

Next, let him resolve to set apart for reading *in course* a due proportion of the daily period which he can devote to works. Especially should this be done within the department of history, and continued until one has become possessed of clear and connected views of the rise, progress, and succession of the leading nations in the civilized world. At first, perhaps, the attempt at regularity may be found irksome; nevertheless, let not the reader yield to impatience. Better, if need be, that he should begin with only twenty minutes a day, and pursue a course, than to read tenfold that amount in a desultory way. A little, well understood, is worth more than much learned imperfectly: for in the former case the mind keeps what it gets, is enlivened and strengthened; in the latter, it soon loses what it had found, becomes weak, confused, and inert.

A book of reference, like the Encyclopædia Americana, or the Penny Cyclopædia, is quite necessary in almost every kind of reading, but especially in the historical.* Next to that in importance, is Anthon's Classical Dictionary; also his system of Ancient and Mediæval Geography. *Blake's* Biographical Dictionary will be found useful in this connection. In perusing the old historians, the names of people and of places with which the reader is not familiar, should be sought out, and their character, as well as their position, should be understood. An Atlas with ancient and modern maps is also a desirable accompaniment. In reading a book like Cæsar's Journal of his Wars in Gaul, the location

* The Encyclopædia Britannica (Edinburgh edition) is the most perfect work of the kind extant; but its cost places it beyond the reach of the majority of readers.

of the tribes of which he speaks should be ascertained. In this way progress may sometimes be slow, but the reward will be rich and lasting.

After reading the history of any particular period, it is a good plan to peruse in connection with it, any good work which may be properly called *pictorial*, giving a dramatic view of the characters of that time. Shakspeare's Julius Cæsar and Addison's Cato may be read with zest even after the briefest history of the downfall of the Roman Republic, and Scott's Kenilworth may profitably succeed an account of the reign of Elizabeth. A similar remark will apply to books of modern travels and researches. With the history of Egypt in Rollin, or in Taylor's Manual, one may well connect Mr. GLIDDON'S recent pamphlet on that country.

In commending these remarks to young readers, the writer is emboldened by the conviction that the course which is marked out in these pages embraces works of standard character and of universal interest. However great the number which may deserve to be added to the list, it is pretty clear that few or none can be spared from it. They are all like "the Everlasting Book" wrought by an ingenious Italian, with leaves of asbestos and letters of gold, suited to defy the ravages of time and of all the elements. The number of volumes too is larger than could be found in the University of Oxford only four centuries ago. And few there are who cannot command as much time as was then allowed to a student for general reading: for in the statutes of St. Mary's College, which was founded in 1446, was the following: "Let no scholar occupy a book in the library above one hour, or two hours at most, so that others be hindered from the use of the same." The aids to reading which are now enjoyed in this country are miracles of art; and "to use as not abusing" them, is one of the first and highest duties of every American.

NOTE A.

OLIVER CROMWELL.

AMONG the interesting characteristics of the present times is the progress of historical criticism. That which passes under the name of history requires much sifting in order to separate the wheat from the chaff. This is a work that demands patience, and the great men who have lived too far in advance of their own age to be understood by their contemporaries, must "bide their time." Within the realm of history the day of judgment comes in the present world, the throne is set, the books are opened, sentence is pronounced, and the saying is verified, "there are first that shall be last, and there are last that shall be first."

These remarks are illustrated in the case of Oliver Cromwell who lived in this world to some purpose, became the chief actor in the heroic age of England, stood forth in his own times the champion of liberty, the friend of the oppressed, the terror of tyrants, and left a name that shall be familiar as a household word to the lips of all generations. Like his friend Roger Williams, the founder of Rhode Island, his views were too broad and magnanimous to be comprehended by the men of his own time, so that those actions which sprung from the highest motives have been attributed to the worst and meanest which narrow minds could devise. This heritage of obloquy has been shared too by his most confidential companion, his Latin Secretary, the most splendid genius of English literature, the "poor, blind schoolmaster, Milton," as he was called by Waller, the courtly poet. These three men of kindred spirit lived and acted with firm faith in that soul-stirring and sublime sentiment, which came from the heart and pen of Milton, in these memorable words: "There will be one day a resurrection of names and reputations, as certainly as of bodies."

Two centuries seem to be a long period for a maligned character to wait for its vindication. Justice moves with "a leaden foot," slow, but sure; and in the court of Historical Justice a century is as one day. Those men are worthy of honor who appear in this court as advocates of truth, defenders of those who have been doomed, as was Christ in the High Priest's palace, to be the victim of false testimony. In our own age the life and opinions of Roger Williams have found able expounders; Judge Story, Mr. Bancroft, and others, also, have earned the thanks of mankind for "bringing forth his righteousness to the light," and in the cause of Cromwell, Thomas Carlyle, Dr. Price, and Mr. Headley, with others whose names deserve honorable mention, have performed those labors of love which it required some degree of moral courage to undertake, and which, being done successfully, constitute, on the whole, a heroic work. The men of the past have been wont to associate the name of Cromwell with those of ambitious warriors and revolutionists; the men of the future will behold it shining in that constellation of noble souls, who formed the "sacramental host" of civil and religious freedom.

NOTE B.

LITERATURE OF THE PULPIT.

In the phrase which we have just written, we have designated one of the noblest and mightiest agencies which has been at work in modern times for the formation of the public character and the moulding of popular opinion. Its very existence is an honor to Christianity. We have old literatures of the heathen ages; the literature of the Court, the School, and of the Forum; but classic Heathendom has bequeathed us no literature in which enlightened and cultivated mind is found addressing itself to the great masses of the people for purposes of moral and religious instruction. It has given us deep philosophies, entertaining histories, soul-stirring orations, and immortal poems; but the fire of its genius gleams out in no order of discourses designed to elevate and bless all classes of society—to bring Wisdom down from the skies to talk with men on themes which concern alike the scholar and the peasant, the monarch and the beggar. It left the great multitude of mankind as "sheep without a shepherd." Between the philosophers and the people there was "a great gulf fixed;" each class had a different religion, and each despised the other.

But on that day when Jesus of Nazareth began his work on earth, the scene was changed. He had sat at the feet of no Aristotle or Gamaliel; he showed no ambition to gain "fit audience from court or Sanhedrim; he counselled not with scholastic Rabbies, but set it forth as the peculiar glory of his mission, that the poor had the gospel preached to them. And the poor intently listened to him; they thronged around him, "they wondered at the gracious words which he spake; and whether he stood on the pavement of Solomon's porch, or on the deck of a boat that lay near the shore, or made a mountain his pulpit, "the common people heard him gladly;" for, he preached to them "as one having authority, and not as the scribes."

Before our Lord left the world, he laid the foundation of a teaching ministry as a permanent institution; and in doing so, he opened in his church the fountain of that Pulpit Literature which has already gone forth in many a branching stream to fertilize the moral deserts of the earth, and which is destined yet to flow abroad in richer abundance, until the last waste of Paganism shall bloom as Eden. The words that are spoken in any one age, by means of the pen and the press become the heritage of all succeeding times. The rugged, rocky knowl of Athens, called Mars' Hill, was one of the pulpits of Paul; the discourse which he uttered there is still going forth through the world on its mission of love; and by it, he being dead, yet speaketh, and will continue to speak to generations yet unborn. That discourse laid Revelation, Nature, Art, and Poetry, under contribution for the attainment of its end, and furnished a fine example of a scholar making rich stores of learning yield their ministry to the glory of the cross. The entrance of the CHRISTIAN SERMON into the field of literary history marks a great moral era, and the Christian church of any period has reason to rejoice, if she find the Pulpit putting forth a power which can cope with the errors of the age, and adapted to meet her own demands for instruction in the truth.

Dr. Williams's Miscellanies, his Sermons on the Lord's Prayer, and on Religious Progress, have been welcomed by many as a permanent addition to the Christian literature of America. It contains discourses called forth by various occasions, which have arisen along the course of the author's ministry; bringing to view, nevertheless, those great, universal principles which suit all times alike, setting them forth in a style of such beauty, grandeur and force, that we may safely declare the book to be one of those which "posterity will not willingly let die." When Archbishop Leighton was asked why he did not, like others, preach "the duties of the times," he replied, "if all the brethren have preached on the *times*, may not one poor brother be suffered to preach on *eternity?* We think, however, that Dr. Williams has looked with a "single eye" at both sides of the matter to which the question pointed, and has preached, at once, both on eternity and the times; irradiating the present by lights which beam from revelations of the future, and drawing from the dread prospects which lie before us, motives that bear right well on the duties of the passing hour.

NOTE C.

WHIPPLE'S LECTURES.

It is not often that we take up a book of Lectures and read it straight through, spell-bound for successive hours, as many remember to have been over the chapters of Macaulay's English history. Generally, we are content, in perusing a volume of discourses, to take one at a time; and it very seldom happens that an address of any kind which is received with popular applause from the lips of a speaker has equal power to command attention when committed to the voiceless page, even though it be helped by all the arts of typography. The orations of Edward Irving charmed the ears of thousands, but they hardly found one reader "to do them reverence."

The lectures of Mr. Whipple, however, were not only received with enthusiasm as they were addressed by the author to the public ear, but have been greeted by the eyes of thousands with a cordial welcome, have engaged the reader's attention from first to last with an unrelaxing energy, and fix their features in his memory in lines not to be erased.

In the use of his powers as a lecturer, and a writer, Mr. Whipple seems to be doing the work for which he was born—for which nature and education have qualified him. He moves serenely in the higher walks of criticism. His step is firm without any air of arrogance. He sees clearly into the heart of things, tells calmly what he sees, and tells it in a way that carries conviction to the mind of the listener. Not only does his glance reach to the core of the objects which he judges, but around all the surfaces, however many-sided; takes within its range both the grand and the minute, and distinguishes at once the essential from the accidental. He has a well-balanced combination of faculties; uniting the power of observing facts with that of broad generalization, keen intuition with logical analysis, strong memory with playful imagination, a serious spirit with a quick susceptibility of the ludicrous, warm sympathies with a moral courage inspired by love of truth, and a mental force which concentrates all his energies at will to bear upon a single point. These are elements of character which form a critic of the highest order; and, whosoever brings all these into healthy exercise, cannot be surpassed in his chosen realm of literature unless by one in whom they act with equal harmony, and a still higher degree of intensity.

But then, in perusing the works of Mr. Whipple, we are struck with the view, not only of the developed harmony of these elements, but also of the intensity of their action. There is not only symmetrical movement, but that movement is full of vitality. He has a heart of fire whose pulsations are regulated by a calm intellect. Hence his writings abound in expressions that are brilliant without glare, poetical without madness, sarcastic without malignity, and strong without extravagance. He has a complete mastery of language. He can make words picture scenes as well as things. His imagery is radiant with vivid colors, but we feel at once that its glow is the refraction of nature's sunlight and not the effect of artificial tints.

These remarks are justified not only by Mr. Whipple's Lectures, but also by his Essays and Reviews, published by the Appletons, in New York and Philadelphia. They will well repay the reader for all the time he may bestow upon them, simply by their power to encourage and stimulate independent thinking, to lift the mind to a point, whence, as from a mountain-eminence, it may survey wide landscapes in the realm of thought, which take in both land and sea—forests, fields, gardens, and arid deserts. In such surveys the young student will prize the aid of one who "*believes* and therefore speaks," who is possessed of a transcendental fancy wedded to Anglo-Saxon common-sense.

The Self-governed Man.

"HE THAT RULETH HIS SPIRIT IS BETTER THAN HE THAT TAKETH A CITY."—Proverbs xvi. 32.

AMONG the fragments of biography which have come down to us from the days of ancient Greece there is a short story of one of the old philosophers that has lighted up a smile on the features of many a schoolboy, while he has been poring over the early lessons of his classics. It is said that Diogenes was seen traversing the market-place in open day with a lighted lamp in his hand. On being asked what was the object of his search, he replied, that he was seeking for a man. However heartily the traffickers, the loungers, and the talkers of the Agora may have ridiculed this eccentric action, they must have felt the point of the keen cynical satire; the veriest trifler must have paused for a moment, at least, to have turned his thoughts to the true idea of manliness, and must have considered the truth that neither outward form, nor garb, nor grace of manner, nor rank, nor wealth, nor learning, were sufficient to constitute a man.

We shall not attempt to discriminate with care the

elements which in the Cynic's view were regarded as essential to true manhood; but probably that radical idea of *power* which inheres in the Anglo-Saxon term from which our English word *man* is derived, was the primary element of his conception. The aim of his philosophy, like that of the Stoic, was to give to the mind the mastery of the senses. His practical discipline was designed to subdue the appetites. A human being ruled by the senses was deemed a mere brute. But a set of healthy faculties under the guidance of an enlightened mind—*power swayed by reason*—this was the leading feature of that ideal standard of character which he sought to realize. When this type of manhood reached its highest point of attainment, it had risen superior to all outward things; it found all its resources within itself; it had little need of material wealth; it could look down upon kings; it was the denizen of the universe. The grandest representation of this mental royalty which pagan history furnishes, was the philosopher of Sinope, who, while residing at Corinth, being asked by the monarch of the world to declare how he might serve him, replied, "Be pleased just to stand a little out of my sunshine." No wonder that the conqueror of empires then felt he had met his match, and exclaimed, "If I were not Alexander, I would be Diogenes."

This stern, lofty virtue of a refined speculative Paganism, lacked one essential element of true humanity, viz., religious philanthropy. I speak of religious philanthropy in distinction from philanthropy as a blind social instinct. Without a clear conception of God, as the universal Father, combining in Himself all that is venerable and lovely; of God as a Supreme Ruler whose laws are sustained by the sanctions of Eternal Majesty, a man can have no real dignity in the sight of his fellow-man; he is the mere chance product of an orphan universe, a transient atom floating in boundless space; and then philanthropy can have no real existence. The word itself may dwell familiarly on the lips, but there is no heart to interpret its meaning; it belongs not to the scenes of actual life, but to the realm of airy abstractions, of poetry or romance. Hence, the virtue produced by the old philosophies was proud and harsh, cold and repulsive; in a word, it was selfish. All its aims, and all its motives, sprang from and terminated in self. This defect Christianity alone could remedy. To do this it was fully adequate. It revealed a Messiah, who, though divine, was nevertheless human; a perfect man; a man in whose character love was the chief vital force, the pervading grace, the crowning perfection. He stands before us a being of majestic power; but that power is ruled by wisdom, and that wisdom is united to god-like love. He breathes new life into our poor humanity; He lifts up the fallen soul; He touches the heart of stone, and it beats with the pulsation of holy sympathy; He reconstructs the shattered character, and every true disciple, newly created in His image, and developed into fulness of stature, walks forth before the world a self-governed man.

Is not such a character a worthy object of our search and study? Does it not far excel any other production of God's handiwork? Wheresoever we behold man of this sterling stamp, whether in the marble palace or the thatched hut, in the camp or the shop, in the senate-chamber or the counting-room, wielding the pen or the hammer, ploughing the deep with his oaken keel or the land with his iron share, clad in fine linen from a foreign loom, or in the coarsest homespun from his own farm, we recognize his imperial brow, and yield him spontaneous homage. We have sometimes seen that lovers of art have crossed oceans and continents to behold what great things have been wrought by the pencil or the chisel of some master hand; and more than one poor student who has fed on bread and water to obtain the means of a journey to Rome has felt himself repaid for all his toils when he has stood before the Apollo of the Vatican. It is an object of thought that enlarges and elevates the mind; and we may truthfully say of the well-formed character, what the celebrated Abbé Winckelmann said of the matchless statue: "Go and study it, and if you see no peculiar beauty in it to captivate you, go again; and if you still discern nothing, go again, and again, and again; for be assured it is there."

It is the sentiment of my text that self-government implies the exercise of a moral power which is itself the highest greatness. Let me ask you, therefore, to proceed with me in directing our thoughts to the *nature of an effective self-government.*

The FIRST point to be observed is, that it involves a just conception of the *object of life.* From what we have seen of the world, it is easy for us to conceive of a young man blest with a noble and a gentle nature, with the highest order of talents, a combination of well-balanced faculties, a sound mind in a healthy body, who, nevertheless, has never given a single moment to the inquiry, What is the design of my existence? In such a case, what avail the most dazzling gifts, or the finest opportunities of culture? He can have no well-defined aim. He is the creature of accidents. He is like a racer who knows not the goal; or a combatant who sees not his antagonist, but with mighty force "beateth the air." Who could behold the richly freighted ship upon the deep, bound to no port, drifting with every current, the sport of wind and wave? Here let it be considered, that one great distinction of human nature is the capacity to form a clear conception of the chief object of life, and to subordinate to its attainment every element of our being. This is the prime attribute of rationality; for it is left to mere animals, impelled by instinct, to eat, drink, sleep, and move hither and thither by blind, unanxious spontaneity. And yet, alas, we have known a pretentious philosopher in the person of a bearded and mustachioed youth, fresh from the university, who, when asked whether his chosen course of living would enable him to attain the true object of life, replied, "I never ask myself so metaphysical a question; I follow my nature, throw the reins upon the neck of the animal, and go whither it leads me." He meant to spend his ample income as a gentlemanly lounger in traversing the whole circuit of the European capitals.

This question, however, relating to the true object of life, is one of more than ordinary pith and moment. It meets us at every turn. To overlook it must be a fatal mistake. An error in regard to it must vitiate every process of reasoning, and cause every step of one's course to deviate from a right line of direction. A caustic remark of John Foster, on a certain class of Miss Edgeworth's literary works—her Tales of Fashionable Life—is quite relevant to the point before us. After reminding his reader that this lady does not profess to write for mere amusement, but for the high purpose of moral teaching, and that she is therefore placed within the reach of a much graver sort of criticism than would at first view appear applicable to a writer of tales, he says: "It is a grand point of incompetency, if an author is totally ignorant of what the human race is made for. And there appears nothing in the present or such other of her works as we have happened to look into, to prevent the surmise that this question would completely baffle her. Reduce her to say what human creatures were made for, and there would be an end of her volubility." Be assured, O Friends, Miss Edgeworth is not alone in this dilemma. Too often have we seen the finest mastery of language, the most charming grace of style, the keenest observation of men and manners, the highest powers of graphical description, even though wedded to great creative genius, all lavished on the veriest trifles. What a spectacle! Powers that range but little below the angelic, engrossed with nursery toys! If in a lunatic asylum you should behold one of your own species, formed by nature to vie with a Washington, or a Wellington, engaged with enthusiastic delight in building card-houses, or discharging toy-guns, the sight would move your pity; yet we need not go far to find the most gifted minds, fitted to adorn any sphere of life, tasked in the pursuit of airy nothings, deaf to all the voices which call to us from the heights and depths of creation, and saying unto each and every one, Press forward to the prize—so run as to obtain.

But I can readily imagine that some friendly reader would fain interpose, and say, Dwell no longer on the importance of the object, but, if you can, declare with all simplicity what it is. Nay; but, O Reader! let me not here assume to be thine oracle; rather will I stand aside and let the great Master speak. The true Messiah, the desire of nations, is revealed. I am come, said he, a Light into the world. For this cause am I come, that I should bear witness unto the truth. Every one that is of the truth heareth my voice. In him, were truth and love incarnated. In him Divine Wisdom dwelt with men, and lived a human life. From him came rays of celestial light, to interweave and incorporate themselves with the elements of humanity. "And I, if I be lifted up," said he, "will draw all men unto me." He has become the grand attracting object of the moral world. He is the Head of a spiritual empire which is every moment extending its bounds. Other empires have risen and passed away, but his must increase; and, as said the exiled Emperor of France on the rock of St. Helena, "He rules by love, and at this hour millions of men would die for him."

Accept his chief gift—the boon of kingly grace; it is *salvation.* Having accepted it, serve him with a heart of gratitude, and "work out your salvation" in serving him. Thus faith becomes developed in the whole sisterhood of virtues. To establish his moral kingdom in the soul, to build it up, as we may, around us, seeking its triumph over all the world—this is the chief aim of a Christian man. This is an object which gives to life some worth, and impresses a real dignity on the minutest actions that have a relation to it. This is an object in the pursuit of which man carries with him the favor of God and the sympathy of all heavenly intelligences. It is an object which demands thought, feeling, inventiveness, and firm resolve; which opens wide scope for all human wisdom and energy; for the use of money, skill, science, influence, exertion; for every sort of talent or acquirement, and for every element of lawful power. It is, therefore, the object to which all human businesses should be made to minister. To this Agriculture should bring its first fruits, Commerce its first tributes, Art its highest achievements, and all departments of life should not only be subordinated to it, but animated and pervaded by its principles and spirit. For a man to become rooted and grounded in these truths, "to grow up into them in all things," is to accomplish his proper life-work upon the earth, and to be preparing for an elevation to that higher sphere to which he shall be welcomed with the plaudit, "Well done; thou hast been faithful over a few things, I will make thee ruler over many things."

In this connection, a SECOND leading truth demands our notice: A wise self-government not only involves a just conception of the main object of life, but also a *fit plan of action.*

A just conception of the object is quite essential to success. But it is not enough that the racer clearly discern the goal; he must conform himself to a plan of discipline that shall secure the subordination of his faculties, appetites, and passions to his chosen end. Just as, of old, he who hoped on the day of combat to win the Olympian laurel, schooled his whole nature into prompt obedience to his will by subjection to a wholesome regimen. He did not despise theories, nor sneer at general principles as mere abstractions. He thoroughly studied them; but having mastered them, *practice* was the word, and gymnastic exercises his employment. Evidently, a young man may have before him a right ideal standard of character, a clear and comprehensive view of his object, and yet fail practically to realize it. He may dream away his life in speculative reveries. He may become the sport of fruitless imaginings. Neglecting the humble duty of the present hour, he may be sighing for opportunities of action. He may be saying within himself, If I were only in this or that profession, if I had this or that man's advantages, I might do my life-work worthily. He may be indulging the erroneous sentiment that occasions make the man; whereas great occasions cannot come every day, and when they do arrive, the man for them is already made.

Now a failure at either of these two points—a right

conception of the object of life, or a well-adjusted plan of action—may be equally fatal to ultimate success. Without the one, there will be no just and noble aim; without the other, the noblest aim cannot be realized. You have seen men in whose honesty of purpose and in whose keen sensibility to honor you have had unshaken confidence, ensnared and overcome by some sudden temptation, entrapped and surprised into the saying or doing of something which would defeat their own deliberate intentions; like Lawrence Hyde, the second son of the Chancellor Clarendon, and First Lord of the Treasury under Charles I., of whom Macaulay says, "Very slight provocations sufficed to kindle his anger; and when he was angry, he said bitter things which he forgot as soon as he was pacified, but which others remembered many years: for nothing was easier than to goad him into a passion; and from the moment he went into a passion, he was at the mercy of opponents far inferior to him in capacity."

Nevertheless, that man had many devoted friends, and was in reality far more estimable than his celebrated associate in office, who was highly gifted with the power of self-control, who could render every faculty subordinate to his aim, even though that aim were of the meanest order, and whose infamy the same descriptive pen has made immortal. "Godolphin," says the historian, "had been bred a page at Whitehall, and had early acquired all the flexibility and the self-possession of a veteran courtier. He was laborious, clear-headed, and profoundly versed in the details of finance. Every government, therefore, found him a useful servant; and there was nothing in his opinions or his character which could prevent him from serving any government." "Sidney Godolphin," says Charles, "is never in the way and never out of the way." This pointed remark goes far to explain Godolphin's extraordinary success in life. "He acted at different times with both the great parties, but he never shared in the passions of either. Like most men of cautious temper and prosperous fortunes, he had a strong disposition to support whatever existed. He disliked revolutions; and for the same reason for which he disliked revolutions, he disliked counter-revolutions. His deportment was remarkably grave and reserved, but his personal tastes were low and frivolous, and most of the time which he could save from public business was spent in racing, card-playing, and cock-fighting." Contrasted examples like these of persons who have occupied conspicuous spheres of action, clearly indicate, on the one hand, that a man whose aim is comparatively elevated sometimes fails of its attainment for the want of a plan of life fitted to secure the right direction of the elements of his power, and, on the other hand, that a man gifted by nature with the finest faculty of self-control may pursue the vilest objects with consummate skill, and may prostitute the most masterly executive talents to the highest bidder in those shambles where Mammon trades in the souls of men.

This observation leads us to a THIRD important truth relating to our subject, namely: that a *vital religious faith* is an essential element of an effective plan of action. In studying the history of those moral heroes whose deeds have shaped the fortunes of the race, who in the accomplishment of their undertakings have coped successfully with great opposing craft and force, who have passed unscathed through fiery ordeals and spurned the most dazzling bribes held out to allure them from their high career, an analysis of their characters has always shown that their strongest incentives and supports were derived from the truths of religion. As the truths were not apprehended by the senses, or by intuition, but chiefly by faith in the Divine testimony, we say that religious faith is an essential element of an effective plan of life. There are times when all propitious influences conspire to bear one onward in his chosen course, and he moves as at the beck of destiny; but there are also times which try the soul, which search, test, and prove it, and discern "what manner of spirit" rules within. There are times when external aids all fail, when the Power of Darkness has its hour, when temptations start up suddenly so as to impel to instant decision, and the man is thrown back on those interior principles that form the ground-work of character. To the array of outward evils there can be no counterpoise except in the motives furnished by religion. Even Voltaire, heartless as he was, and prone to mock at every thing sacred, had an intellectual eye, keen enough to perceive the truth of this in relation to the government of States, and therefore declared that unless there be diffused among the people a prevailing belief in an invisible and omniscient Power, taking cognizance of secret as well as overt actions, a Power to whom the darkness and the light were both alike.

all law must become inefficacious. Now we affirm that the principle which he was so willing to apply to the body politic reaches farther still, and that while a sound religious belief is essential to the existence of a well-governed State, it is equally essential to the existence of a well-governed man.

Hence, whenever the religious faith of a people becomes corrupt, whether it be through the want of a healthy freedom, as is the case in Europe, or through the abuse of freedom, as is too likely to be the case in America, the foundations of private virtue become sapped and undermined. This defect is brought to light, first of all, in the infidelities and alienations that mar the peace of domestic circles; then in the trickeries of trade which desecrate the intercourse of the commercial community; next, in those startling crimes of great defaulters which send thrills of agony through all ranks of society; and finally, in the languor and decay of the state itself. Pregnant with meaning in illustration of this point, is a short paragraph from the pen of Gibbon touching the decline and fall of the Roman Empire: "In their writings and conversations the philosophers of antiquity asserted the independent dignity of reason, but they resigned their actions to the commands of law and custom. Viewing with a smile of pity and indulgence the various errors of the vulgar, they diligently practised the ceremonies of their fathers; devoutly frequented the temples of the gods; and sometimes, condescending to act a part on the theatre of superstition, they concealed the sentiments of an atheist under the sacerdotal robes. Reasoners of such a temper were scarcely inclined to wrangle about their respective modes of faith or worship. It was indifferent to them what shapes the folly of the multitude might choose to assume; and they approached with the same inward contempt and the same external reverence the altars of the Lybian, the Olympian, or the Capitoline Jupiter." In a state of public sentiment which renders religion merely conventional, the manly virtues can never flourish; and in the individual or the community, the eclipse of faith will surely be followed by the blight of every element of self-preserving power.

Now let it be observed that truly akin to this fashionable irreligion of the days of the Antonines is, the fashionable irreligion of the nineteenth century which aims to enrobe itself in forms of Christian philosophy, and which has already spoken to the cultivated classes of American society from the pages of the pamphlet and the magazine, the stately quarterly and the elaborate volume, in lectures of the lyceum and in discourses from the pulpit. It inscribes the word "progress" on its banner and its symbols. It would repel with quiet scorn the imputation of atheism; nay, it teaches that the universe itself is but Deity developed; that He lives and moves in every thing that is; in all matter, in all spirit; for all these and we ourselves are but parts of Him. Therefore, every thing is good; all matter, all spirit; evil is only good seen on the wrong side; and just as carrion resolves itself into the bloom and flower of vernal vegetation, so, by an eternal law of progress, man, whether he be now found in the palace or the prison, the church or the brothel, is moving forward to loftier and wider spheres of joyous existence.

This subtle theology furnishes such ample scope for the adoration of nature under the name of God, for eloquent tributes of homage to the Deity, and for the poetry of devotion, that to many minds it has seemed to be invested with an air of piety. But then, it so thoroughly confounds the Creator with his works, God with man, the holy with the vile, it looks so exclusively at God as a universal Cause and denies his being as a Lawgiver, that it must practically erase from the mind every feeling of accountability, and must subvert, in the end, all distinction between right and wrong, good and evil, the holy and the sinful. This old oriental pantheism, this religious philosophy, so long known in Europe as the theology of Spinosa, has no aspect of novelty except that which invests it from the circumstance of its being taught in New England, christened with sacred names, adapted to the apprehension of the common mind, couched in pithy maxims, and wedded to the arts of poetry, music, and song. But let this doctrine, which is already welcomed in certain highly-cultivated circles, become prevalent among the youth of this land, become inwrought with the primary elements of their belief, so as to work itself out in the formation of character, and then to cherish the grave expectation of their standing forth a race of self-governed men would be the "height of the ridiculous." A young man with such a theory of religion may be familiar with all the practical wisdom of Solomon's Proverbs, with all the oracles of the Grecian sages, the terse lines of Lacon, and the sayings of Poor Richard; but in the hour of temptation, in the keen struggle with enticing forms of sin, these would all fall asunder like threads of flax at touch of fire. Instead of feeling the restraint of the divine law, and schooling his passions into subjection to it, he would, of necessity, in times of excitement, follow the lowest, because they are the strongest impulses of his nature; and throwing the reins upon the neck of appetite, would swear that he was only obeying the Deity who lives and rules within him. Thus would vice turn holy "put religion on;" and to him, as to the young Roman who invoked the gods to be propitious to his nights of lawless lust, the vilest crimes would be invested with the sanctions of divinity. No form of atheism could reach a more fatal issue; and it would appear at last that the schools which nourish the principles of this sort of transcendental philosophy are, to use an expression of the Prophet Isaiah, "hatching cockatrices' eggs;" hastening to produce the vipers that fascinate the eye with their glittering colors, their fleet and graceful movements, but whose touch is poison, and whose sting is mortal. Its development might be slow, but it would be sure. Like those seeds which, taken out of Egyptian mummies wherein they had lain two thousand years, when planted in the earth took root and flowered, so, an erroneous principle in religion, though it may seem harmless while enwrapped with the bandages of old forms, customs, and opinions, yet, falling at last in some genial soil, will put forth its life, and produce "its vines which are vines of Sodom, and its grapes which are grapes of gall."

Young man, friend and brother! Although I am a stranger to the incidents that make up your personal history; although I have no faculty of clairvoyance which enables me to penetrate the inner chamber of your thoughts, yet I doubt not that could I follow you to scenes of retirement, and listen to the musings of your solitude, and daguerreotype upon the tablet of memory the varying moods of your spirit, I could hold up to your recognizing eye the impressions of many moments in which the ideal pictures of a manly, Christian, and nobly self-governed character have detained your attention, have charmed your imagination, and awakened the resolve to aim at their realization in actual life. Now and then success has seemed possible; perhaps easy. But experience has made a mockery of your hopes. Defeat and failure have brought over you a painful sense of impotence. The remembrance of fruitless resolutions has fanned the fires of remorse. Then you have been tempted to bring down your ideal standard to the low level of prevailing custom—to deny the possibility of Christian virtue, to decline the contest with evil, to drift with the current of fashion, and to be content with the amiable but vain wish for a better state of things, in which the syren-like temptations that beset your path shall have been swept away from around you. It is not strange if experience should already have taught you by its rough handling in such a way as to qualify you to feel the tremendous truthfulness to nature and to fact which quivered in the expression of one who, having unfolded to me the workings of his struggling heart, exclaimed, "If I were owner of a million sterling, and by laying it at your feet I could be transformed into a true Christian, I would do it cheerfully; and yet, before to-morrow, I may be enticed away by two shillings' worth of sin!" Strange indeed would it be if there were not many who can deeply sympathize with this appalling sense of moral weakness.

Say now, whether, for a case like this, there may be found on earth an adequate redeeming power? No question that ever came from mortal lips can have a more far-reaching practical significance than this. How shall I frame my speech so as to impress the true answer on every mind? I will not attempt to do it by abstract propositions or formal arguments. Let me cite an incident of biography which carries with it a volume of illustration. In a garden at Milan, in the year 372, amidst the bloom and fragrance of the opening spring, a young man might have been seen one day reclining under a tree, his face bathed in tears, his mind agonized with recollections of his wasted life. Scenes of sensual revelry filled the whole retrospect of bygone years. Crushed with a painful sense of self-degradation, and of the utter impossibility of permanent reform, he deeply groaned in spirit. A youthful voice reached his ear. Whence it came he knew not. Whether the excitement of his own soul invested a sudden thought with a power that made it seem vocal, or whether it was one of those strange coincidences of outward events which Divine Providence sometimes brings about, we cannot tell; but that voice uttered a sentence apposite to his condition. It said, "Tolle, lege; tolle, lege,"—Take and read; take and read. That sentence brought to his remembrance a parchment roll that he had just held in his hand while in a neighboring arbor. He hastened back, took up the roll, and read the first lines that met his eye. That roll was Paul's Epistle to the Romans; those lines were what we now designate as the two closing verses of the thirteenth chapter: "Let us, therefore, cast off the works of darkness, and let us put on the armor of light. Let us walk honestly, as in the day; not in rioting and in drunkenness; not in chambering and wantonness; not in strife and envying; but put ye on the Lord Jesus Christ, and make not provision for the flesh to fulfil the lusts thereof." Those words were words of power. They wounded and they healed. That hour was the turning-point of a history, the commencement of a glorious career. From that hour Augustine became another man; for ten centuries his was the leading name of Christendom; his works now form an important part of ancient literature, and through them, in spite of many errors of opinion pertaining to his times, he still keeps his hold upon the memories and affections of the passing age. Where now lay the secret of this illustrious change of character? Simply in the joyous welcome with which faith hailed the revelation of a personal Saviour—that divine Messiah who then arose upon his delighted vision as the star of an eternal day.

Having thus exhibited the nature of self-government; having shown that it requires a just conception of the true object of life, with a well-adjusted plan of action, and that a vital Christian faith is an essential element of such a plan, it may be proper now to suggest a few hints bearing upon the realization of these ideas in actual life. Apart from these principles, mere rules and practical maxims must be all in vain. But if the mind be impressed with the worth of these cardinal truths, and if the heart be disposed to welcome them, then all those hints in which are stored the wisdom of experience may find ample scope and play, because there is within the man himself a moral power that is competent to apply them.

(1.) The first which I shall venture to suggest in this connection is, that every one should learn to regard with close attention and manly honesty his own faults and weaknesses. This is a thing which is verily easily said, but a thing very hard to accomplish. You have, doubtless, seen many high-souled Christian men who were incapable of a wicked deed, yet unconsciously cherishing the most egregious faults. I have heard one and another of this class of persons say with the bland and winning tones of confidential friendship, "Tell me of my faults;" but where is the friend who will venture to affront your self-esteem by calling your attention to what he knows to be a petted and protected weakness? Ay; be assured that in the view of any one who values your good-will this is rather a risky business, and he fears that it will not pay. It is easy to play about the surface of the character with light and gentle touches, but no one can point out a real fault without inflicting mental pain. It is impossible for you or me to do it for another "in good earnest," without a resolution as firm and energetic as that of the surgeon who would straighten a crooked limb or set a disjointed finger. But if the subject of such an operation regard the blemish as a peculiar beauty, a wise friend may find himself as much obliged to handle charily the faults of the living as he is to "tread lightly on the ashes of the dead." Self-love blinds us all, and we naturally hate the pain of self-discipline. If you have ever chanced to visit the studio of a successful sculptor, it is likely that you have gazed with rapture on some noble work still under the master's hand, and have been enchanted with its loveliness of form, so that it seemed as if the marble breathed; just as in years gone by I have stood by Hiram Powers in his laboratory at Florence, watching the artist's movements while he was dealing the finishing strokes on a work of matchless beauty, and thought if the statue were endowed with sensation with what entreating tones it would utter its appeal against these superfluous chisellings; but then, he who would attain a manly character, standing forth in well-poised and truthful symmetry, must learn to bear the edge of sharp rebuke, and welcome the hand that would rasp it into those fair proportions that will endure the scrutiny of friend or foe.

(2.) Cultivate those simple tastes, those unostentatious personal qualities which are generally known by the descriptive name of *home-bred* virtues, and which always throw an abiding charm around the scenes of domestic and social life. They include those elements of social excellence which the French designate by the phrase "les petites morales." These relate not merely to the government of the appetites and passions, but of the tongue and the temper, the habitual expressions of the countenance and the tones of voice, to modes of speech and to courtesies of intercourse, which too many despise as little things beneath their notice, but which, nevertheless, sustain such important relations to character and life as to verify the scriptural proverb, "He that despiseth little things shall fall by little and little."

This rule implies the cultivation of a certain quality which is an element of beauty in all things, namely, *simplicity;* it inculcates simplicity of manners and habits, style of living and personal appearance. On the one hand, it would guard against the silly ambition of the young rowdy who affects coarseness and vulgarity; on the other hand, it would guard against the foolish vanity of the dandy who affects refinement, and supposes that a fashionable tailor can impart all that is essential to a gentleman. These two characters, occupying opposite extremes in the social scale sustain each other; just as we sometimes see that "rogues in rags are kept in countenance by rogues in ruffles."

This cultivation of simple tastes implies the love of substance and reality rather than of surface shows and mere appearances. In some families you will find, apparently, all the means of enjoyment accumulated with unstinted munificence, and every thing that wealth can furnish is made to minister to the attainment of happiness: sculpture, painting, and the scientific arts have all been tasked to produce works of beauty; the soft tones of the piano, harp, or guitar, court the ear; but you will listen in vain for the music of the soul, for the harmony of voices attuned to the utterance of kindly affections and truthful sentiments; in a word, you look in vain for scenes glowing with the quiet charms of a well-ordered *home.* "This also is vanity and vexation of spirit." Better is a dinner of herbs in the lath and plaster cottage where truth and goodness reign, than the meat of stalled oxen in the lordly mansion where there is no communing of kindred souls and where hearts know no rest.

(3.) Let it be our aim to regulate our natural love of excitement; to *regulate* it, I say, for it can never be extirpated. And by regulating it, I mean the giving it an active direction towards its proper objects. The love of excitement is implanted by nature in almost every sensitive being. Every thing that hath breath finds a joyous excitement in the exercise of its active powers. Throughout the wide realm of animated nature there is a constant alternation of action and repose; and there is no more interesting proof of the benevolence of God in the physical universe, than may be seen in the thrilling pleasures which all the lower tribes experience in the employment of their faculties. The little insect dancing through the sunny air, the bee flying to find her food in the bosom of every flower, the bird soaring to hail the morning with her song, the lamb leaping sportively around the fold, the hound bounding over the field at his master's call, the horse whose neck is "clothed with thunder" pawing the earth in the pride of his strength, all show that fine susceptibility of excitement which springs from the conscious joy of a sensitive nature. The little child also exhibits it before the intellect is at all developed; and then, having added strength to strength, he tasks his parent's mind to meet this demand by toys and sports and projects of useful exercise. If, with advancing years, his tastes can be rightly directed so that they shall find gratification for this love of excitement in healthful pursuits, in the acquisitions of literature and science, in an honest business, in honorable and improving associations, in promoting the interests of religion and humanity, then it answers its true design. Then, one may have by nature as much of excitable energy, and as much of fondness for society as distinguished a William Wilberforce or a William Wirt, yet it will all be kept in healthy action, and be made to subserve the aims of a useful life. But, on the other hand, if this love of excitement have no moral regulation, if it become the sport of accident, and be left to its own wild and fitful moods, there is no telling what course it may take or with what vile objects it may be gratified. At any rate, it sweeps away every thing that opposes it with the might of a hurricane and mocks at the voice of reason. In savage life, even before the white man carried the strong alcohol, the Indian would seek relief from vacancy by the inebriation of noxious weeds and by contriving the most disgusting modes of intoxication. And here amongst ourselves you may trace the operation of the same principle, if at some time in the social haunts of a country village or at a corner of the streets in the great city, you will observe a group of boys who shall have met to while away their evening hours; and after their stock of news and stories have failed to gratify their longing for excitement, see them move off to some bar-room or saloon, just to draw from the intoxicating glass that hilarity which relieves the pain of a vacant mind preying upon itself. Thenceforward their moral ruin proceeds apace. The attachments of home perish. Social life is prized chiefly because it feeds a morbid love of excitement, and when that becomes the peculiar charm and power of society, the most dissipated class will, ere long, be preferred, and by degrees character will gravitate to the lowest abyss of degradation.

But thanks be to God! Notwithstanding the temptations that beset us, and the strength of our evil inclinations, the gospel reveals a remedy that is adapted to all our moral wants. A childlike faith in that word of everlasting life confers a power which puts a man in possession of himself; enables his weak reason to

> —— break the fiery passions to the bit,
> And, spite of their licentious sallies, keep
> The radiant track of glory;

enables him to subordinate every element of his condition to the grand design of his creation, and to make the great and the minute events of daily life minister to his fitness for nobler realms of bliss, honor, and immortality.

www.ingramcontent.com/pod-product-compliance
Lightning Source LLC
LaVergne TN
LVHW010231110826
845151LV00004B/1259
* 9 7 8 1 4 2 5 5 2 5 3 9 2 *